EDUCATION
COUNTS

An Indicator System to Monitor the Nation's Educational Health

Report of the
Special Study Panel on Education Indicators
to the
Acting Commissioner of Education Statistics

September 1991

NATIONAL CENTER FOR EDUCATION STATISTICS

U.S. Department of Education
Lamar Alexander
Secretary

Office of Educational Research and Improvement
Diane Ravitch
Assistant Secretary

National Center for Education Statistics
Emerson J. Elliott
Acting Commissioner

September 1991

For sale by the U.S. Government Printing Office
Superintendent of Documents, Mail Stop: SSOP, Washington, DC 20402-9328
ISBN 0-16-035838-8

LETTER OF TRANSMITTAL

July 1991

Emerson J. Elliott
Acting Commissioner of Education Statistics
Washington, D.C.

Dear Mr. Commissioner:

The Hawkins-Stafford Elementary and Secondary School School Improvement Amendments of 1988 (P.L. 100-297) authorized the establishment of a Special Study Panel on Education Indicators. This panel was chartered by the Department of Education in July 1989 and directed to prepare a final report, including recommendations, for your consideration and transmission to the Congress of the United States.

On behalf of my colleagues on the panel, I am pleased to report that we have concluded our deliberations and to submit this final report.

Among the panel's major charges was the request to examine: (1) models of educational systems; (2) criteria for selecting educational indicators; (3) a publication of the National Center for Education Statistics (NCES), entitled *The Condition of Education*; (4) data needs and collection efforts; and (5) an indicator development plan for NCES defining recommended indicators and recommending new research and data collection activities. We believe *Education Counts* fully discharges the panel's responsibilities.

I do want to point out the remarkable diversity of interests and experience represented on this panel. The panel includes parents, chief state school officers, school superintendents, principals, teachers, business leaders, and representatives from a variety of academic disciplines. What struck me as unique about its membership when I agreed to chair the panel was the extraordinary cross-section of people serving on it. They represent people on the front line who both educate and employ our young people. My hope was that this diverse group could unite to present a common agenda for your consideration. That hope has been fully realized.

I speak for all members of the panel in expressing our appreciation for your confidence in our ability to complete this important work. On behalf of my colleagues on the panel, I want also to express our gratitude to the able and hard-working staff which helped us in our work. Study director John Ralph, in particular, was unflagging in his dedication to this demanding task and his commitment to seeing it to a successful conclusion.

The members of the panel stand ready to help you in any way we can to help make this document's recommendations a reality.

Respectfully,

Alan D. Morgan
Chairman

CONTENTS

PART I

EDUCATION COUNTS

EDUCATION COUNTS

This report is divided into two major sections. Part I is complete in itself. It presents the panel's overall conception of how an indicator information system should be developed and concludes with recommendations for improvements in federal data collection and reporting in six major issue areas. Part I includes the information of direct interest to most general readers, educators, policymakers, and business leaders.

Part II presents much more detailed information about the six issue areas. It is designed to provide analysts and researchers with more substantive guidance on each of the six issue areas, to identify existing data sources, and to cite gaps in the data and information currently available.

Chapter 1

INTRODUCTION

Education counts in the United States. It counts because every element of personal well-being, social progress, and economic development is bound inextricably to knowledge, learning, and skill. At the deepest level of the individual and collective lives of all Americans, education *matters*.

Education also counts in the sense that our society has to pay attention to it and measure its outcomes and benefits. But in counting the outcomes of education, it is easy to reverse ends and means. The intention is benign: Because we value education we should measure it. But the unintended effect is deceptive: We begin to value only what we *can* measure. Eventually our hopes for what education can become are reduced to numbers, impressive in their apparent precision but silent on the essential meaning of learning in a free society. This panel believes that some things in American education (e.g., funding, graduation rates, and student achievement) can be measured relatively easily, if crudely. But other aspects of the educational enterprise (e.g., how ready our children are for school, how equitably educational opportunities are distributed, and how the larger culture affects learning) are equally important. Because education counts in these ways too, the effort to measure the enterprise must take them into account.

Since the Special Study Panel on Education Indicators first met in November 1989, two potentially historic events have underlined how much education matters in America. Early in 1990, the President and the nation's governors agreed on six goals for American education. In April 1991, President Bush and the Secretary of Education announced a new national education strategy (AMERICA 2000) designed to achieve those goals. Clearly, a national consensus has crystallized around the importance of improving American schools and colleges and raising the level of achievement of their graduates. Public support for education has rarely been higher.

Goals and strategies are statements of national purpose. The six goals are ambitious. The strategy embedded in AMERICA 2000 is broad. Together, they combine to draw the public's attention to a broad array of problems and opportunities in American schools, in preschool preparation, in adult education, and in the "other 91%"—the time between birth and age 18 that students spend outside the classroom. The education goals and AMERICA 2000 intersect with the work of this Special Study Panel in the following way: As a practical matter, neither the federal government, states, nor localities have the systems in place to tell the American people whether the goals have been achieved or the strategy is working.

As a practical matter, neither the federal government, localities, nor states can tell whether the goals have been achieved or the strategy is working.

This document is about what is required in order to create those systems. It is organized not around the education goals, or AMERICA 2000—although it can serve their ends—but around enduring questions of how well our schools and colleges function, our students learn, and our communities support education. This report grows from our belief that, if the broad reform movement is to succeed, the United States must develop a *comprehensive education indicator information system* capable of monitoring the health of the enterprise, identifying problems, and illuminating the road ahead. Without such a system, reform cannot be sustained because, lacking a reliable means of charting progress, it will have to rely on inadequate data and poorly conceived analyses.

The members of this panel—teachers, analysts, school administrators, employers, and academics from across the nation— began their work encouraged by the energy of the nationwide commitment to improve education. We were impressed with several existing efforts to develop a small number of reliable indicators of the nation's educational performance. We were asked to define what those specific indicators should be.

But as our work proceeded, we became convinced that the search for a limited number of key education indicators is misguided. Because no limited set of indices can do justice to the complexity of the educational enterprise, a limited set would not only reflect an educational agenda, they would *define* an educational agenda. If the nation agrees that mathematics and geography are important enough to warrant their own "indicator," but music and foreign languages are not, educators will respond. If the nation convinces itself that it needs indicators of educational expenditures or of student achievement, but not indicators of expenditures on, and achievement levels of, particular groups of disadvantaged school and college students, we run the risk of ignoring significant education problems.

The strength of indicators, in short, is that they focus attention on critical issues. This focusing property means that they can become levers for change; indicators, by themselves, can become tools of reform because they are such excellent devices for public communication. But the focusing property is also their potential weakness: If a limited number of indicators focuses attention on the wrong issues, we may create more educational problems than we solve.

Indicators not only reflect an educational agenda, they define an educational agenda.

Moreover, many other expert groups—a presidentially-appointed National Education Goals Panel, the Secretary of Labor's Commission on Achieving Necessary Skills (SCANS), the governing board of the National Assessment of Educational Progress, the Council of Chief State School Officers, and the President's AMERICA 2000 effort—are already at work defining means to assess educational outcomes of critical importance to their aims (see box on following page). Their work illustrates both the importance of this panel's charge and the dilemma the panel faces: Whose aims do we endorse? Which goals do we accept? Whose vision of education is most compelling? Simply to pose these questions is to answer them: The aims of all these groups are desirable because all address significant aspects of education in the United States.

NATIONAL EDUCATION GOALS AND "AMERICA 2000"

America's Education Goals

By the year 2000:

1. All children in America will start school ready to learn.

2. The high school graduation rate will increase to at least 90 percent.

3. American students will leave grades four, eight, and twelve having demonstrated competency in challenging subject matter including English, mathematics, science, history, and geography [and leave school] prepared for responsible citizenship, further learning, and productive employment in our modern world.

4. U.S. students will be first in the world in science and mathematics achievement.

5. Every adult American will be literate and will possess the knowledge and skills necessary to compete in a global economy and exercise the rights and responsibilities of citizenship.

6. Every school in America will be free of drugs and violence and will offer a disciplined environment conducive to learning.

America 2000

In support of those goals, President Bush announced in April 1991 a four-part strategy:

1. For Today's Students: Better and More Accountable Schools.

2. For Tomorrow's Students: A New Generation of American Schools.

3. For the Rest of Us (Yesterday's Students): A Nation of Students.

4. Communities Where Learning Can Happen.

This realization drives this panel's perspective on education indicators. After more than a year of study and reflection, the panel concludes that a very different concept of indicators is required in American education. Education indicators should be developed to provide information for all parties with a stake in the education discussion—teachers, parents, administrators, employers, and policymakers. The panel, therefore, argues for a far more comprehensive array of indicators than is contemplated by most of the indicator development activities now underway.

Although we argue that the public's legitimate interest in education cannot be met with a few key indicators, that interest will be overwhelmed by hundreds of discrete, unrelated, bits and pieces of information. Indicators must be comprehensive, yet disciplined enough to be manageable. And they must be presented in such a way that various publics can understand them. To summarize the panel's recommendations, we call for an indicator system disciplined by a framework of enduring issues, with the results presented regularly to the public by interpretive reports that place data and analyses within the context of accessible written essays. The panel calls this system an education indicator information system.

The panel believes the system outlined in this document can generate high quality data and analyses about most of the significant issues in American education. Properly developed, it can provide what we call "clusters of indicators" around major issues and concepts affecting American schools, colleges, and students. It can be used by policymakers responsible for defining the nation's education agenda to monitor the education outcomes they consider most significant. And it can be an essential tool for educators and parents interested in exploring how to improve performance.

If a limited number of indicators focuses attention on the wrong issues, we may create more educational problems than we solve.

SIGNIFICANCE OF ISSUE AREAS

The panel strongly recommends that indicators be organized around major issue areas of significant and enduring educational importance. This document defines six major issue areas. Chapter 2 describes these six and explores their relationship to the national education goals. In this introduction, the panel wishes simply to explain why it chose an approach grounded in issues, as opposed to other possible organizing principles.

An issue-oriented approach appeared essential for several reasons. First, most members of the panel have serious reservations about the wisdom of relying exclusively on the major theoretical model used to justify indicator development in the past, namely a model focusing on a triumvirate of "educational inputs-educational processes-educational outputs." Most panelists view this approach as flawed because it encourages the view that the education system produces "products" by taking various raw materials (e.g., students or resources) and processing them in schools. Such a model may seriously mislead decisionmakers if it encourages school "improvement" in ways that create solutions for the wrong problems.

Second, although another model for indicator development—general goals-specific objectives-measurement (i.e., the model explicitly embedded in the statement of national goals)—appeared promising, the panel ultimately rejected it. However useful this model is for defining goals, it is largely oriented toward policies subject to change. An indicator system organized around today' s goals cannot respond to tomorrow's.

Third, the panel hoped to create an issues-oriented indicator system incorporating essential aspects of a "system": It would be comprehensive and complete in itself, incorporating enough fundamental ideas, priorities, and concepts to allow the public to appreciate interconnected aspects of the educational enterprise. On the other hand, the panel does not pretend to have the last word on indicator development. The six issue areas selected by the panel—and the concepts and sub-concepts underlying them—can be thought of as a series of ideas that should anchor national thinking not only about indicators but about education in general.

An indicator system organized around today's goals cannot respond to tomorrow's.

Finally, perhaps most importantly, indicators developed around properly chosen major issues offer an inherent advantage as a means of communicating essential information to the public. Indicator information can serve the needs of educators, or of policymakers, or of the research, analysis, or business communities. But the panel believes that indicators will fail if they do not fulfill their potential to inform the general public about the quality of the educational enterprise. Indicators organized around major educational issues offer many advantages: They provide the opportunity to capture for the public large and enduring educational themes. They can stir debate and discussion. They should provoke thought and controversy. Above all they can add depth and breath to the public's understanding of some of the most important social institutions in the United States, the nation's schools and colleges.

Chapter 2

THE SEARCH FOR EDUCATION INDICATORS

When the National Commission on Excellence in Education declared in April 1983 that "the nation is at risk," it based its conclusion on international comparisons of student achievement completed 10 years earlier and the results of college entrance examinations taken by less than one-third of all high school seniors. The findings, and the stark conclusion drawn from them, helped vault education to the top of the nation's domestic agenda.

One year later, the Secretary of Education unveiled an annual "Wall Chart." Billed as a collection of *education indicators,* the Wall Chart presented statistics comparing states on a number of dimensions, including students' SAT or ACT scores, graduation rates, teachers' salaries, pupil-teacher ratios, expenditures, and characteristics of the student population. The chart was greeted with headlines throughout the country, and with the charge that it was unfair because it used inappropriate measures for comparison purposes.

The conclusions of the Excellence Commission and the indicators presented annually in the Wall Chart have forced educators, citizens, and policymakers to confront a nearly endless series of difficult questions:

- How well are our students doing?
- How do they compare with students from other lands?
- How well-qualified are our teachers?
- How much are we spending and what are we receiving in return?
- What is being taught and how is it taught?
- How many students complete high school and college and what do they do afterward?
- What differences exist among ethnic groups in terms of expenditures, exposure to subject matter, and levels of achievement—and what can we do about them?

Asking the questions is easy. Answering them is hard work. Above all, policymakers have asked: "Why can't we develop a collection of education indicators, comparable to economic or health care indices, to provide snapshots of our educational progress?" The answer to that question is that we can. The effort will take some time. It will require energy and commitment. Above all, it will require understanding what is involved in the development and collection of indicator information, and deciding to put into place a systematic effort to collect the data required.

WHAT IS AN INDICATOR?

There is no educational "Dow Jones" average.

An indicator is a statistic that measures our collective well-being. A genuine indicator measures the health of a system—the economic system, the employment system, the health care system, or the educational system. The consumer price index and unemployment indices are considered reliable indicators within their respective contexts. There are no comparable single indicators of the educational enterprise, much less an educational "Dow Jones" average.

Unlike most other statistics, an indicator is policy-relevant and problem-oriented; it provides information about a significant feature of the system; it usually incorporates a standard against which to judge progress or regression. Life-expectancy figures, for example, indicate a large gap in life expectancy between black and white Americans, a gap that is today growing after decades of narrowing. This indicator has generated renewed attention to the health care and other needs of minority Americans.

Frequently, an indicator can be contrasted with itself over time, and with other indicators if measurement is consistent. To use the examples above once more, the CPI, unemployment rates, and the Dow Jones average are most valuable when results are considered across time to answer questions such as: "Is inflation rising?" "Are more people unemployed than 12 months ago?" "Has the stock market gone up or down this month?" Indeed, the answers to these questions are often combined and contrasted with each other in an effort to plumb the complexities of the nation's economy.

But indicators *cannot,* by themselves, identify causes or solutions and should not be used to draw conclusions without other evidence. Diagnosis is not the function of an indicator just as it is not the function of a temperature gauge in an automobile. The gauge monitors the cooling system and warns the driver if the engine is overheating. But the gauge does not *diagnose* the cause, a task that can easily tax the skill of a highly trained mechanic. An education indicator system can help the public monitor the health of the educational enterprise, but diagnosis and prescription will tax the ingenuity of analysts and researchers.

This brief description presents educators with the task of developing indicators that can: monitor the health of the educational enterprise; provide policy-relevant, problem-oriented information; and generate information that can be compared with itself over time. That task represents a formidable agenda; fortunately, the nation is not starting from scratch. A considerable amount of relevant work is already in progress to help realize the promise of indicators for American education.

PROGRESS TO DATE

A number of organizations and institutions are actively pursuing the search for indicator information. Although these individual efforts do not represent the full richness of what needs to be put in place, collectively they represent a promising beginning. The "Education Summit," convened by the President for the nation's governors in 1989, led to six national goals for education ranging from preschool readiness to participation in the workforce. A panel appointed by the President has taken on the challenge of advancing these goals and developing report cards to assess progress toward them. Several individual states, as part of this effort, have developed complementary goals of their own.

Similarly, the Secretary's Commission on Achieving Necessary Skills (SCANS), appointed by the Secretary of Labor, is in the process of defining skills required in the high-performance workplace of the future—broad areas of workplace competence such as the management of resources, time, and people, and intellectual skills such as reading,

13

writing, mathematics, and problem-solving. A major task of the SCANS commission is assessing student mastery of these skills.

In addition to these new efforts a number of other promising developments have been under way for some time:

- Internationally, the Organization for Economic Cooperation and Development (OECD) plans to report education indicators for 20 countries in 1991. The International Association for the Evaluation of Educational Achievement (IEA) has been measuring student achievement for two decades and provides rich comparative data.

- At the federal level, several longstanding efforts can be drawn on. NCES publishes an annual report, *The Condition of Education,* which provides national data on nearly 50 indicators of elementary, secondary, and postsecondary education. The Department of Education's Wall Chart annually compared states on a variety of measures. The National Science Foundation is developing a biennial Science Education Indicators effort.

- The Council of Chief State School Officers (CCSSO) has initiated an effort to develop "fair and constructive" comparisons among states on characteristics such as demographics and resources, policies and practices, instructional time, student needs, and reform efforts.

- The National Governors' Association (NGA) uses indicators to monitor the states' progress toward reform goals adopted by NGA in 1986 and reports its findings in an annual report *Results in Education.*

- Many states have launched indicator efforts of their own.

- Policy Analysis for California Education (PACE), an independent research center supported by three universities (Berkeley, Stanford, and Southern California), issues an annual "Conditions of Education" report on statewide education trends.

- Several business organizations including the Business-Higher Education Forum, the Business Roundtable, the Committee for Economic Development, and the National Alliance of Business have begun to track education developments of interest to their constituents.

OBSTACLES AHEAD

The efforts already in place are promising. But they fall far short of representing a comprehensive system that is capable of producing policy-relevant, problem-oriented indicators that can measure the health of the education system. Enormous technical obstacles stand between where we are today and that goal. These obstacles include lack of agreement on a conceptual model of an optimally functioning education system, problems with validity and reliability, difficulty ensuring fairness in the use of indicators for comparison purposes, the burden of developing and implementing an indicator system, and the possibility that indicators may be "corrupted."

Lack of Agreement

Agreeing on a set of measures to describe the health of the education system requires broad consensus on how the various pieces of the system fit together. That consensus is elusive and certainly does not exist at present. Given the diverse perspectives on education in the United States, the task of obtaining broad agreement on what constitutes "good educational health" promises to be daunting.

Until 1987, states employed a dozen different methods of reporting school enrollments.

Validity and Reliability

Serious technical problems with the indicators currently available, combined with large gaps in available data sources, pose formidable problems to the construction of an indicator system at the national level. These problems are probably even more severe at the state and local level. CCSSO, at the request of NCES, has focused on deficiencies in comparable outcome measures across reporting units, noting for example that until 1987 states employed at least ten different ways of counting schools and about a dozen different methods of reporting school enrollments. Dropout figures are notoriously unreliable and represent some of the most ambiguous data reported in American education (see box).

THE SEARCH FOR COMPARABLE MEASURES

"According to some national statistics, Georgia's school dropout rate is 37-39%. A recent study completed by researchers at the University of Georgia concludes that it is closer to 18%. How reliable is either statistic? Which is correct?

"The answer is probably both but they cannot be compared. Most dropout numbers are accurate within the context of the definition and time frame used and how data are collected and computed. These vary greatly from state to state, district to district, and organization to organization. Three researchers used 25 different computations taken from cities, districts and states around the country to calculate the Austin, Texas school district's dropout rate. The study yielded 15 different statistics ranging from 10.1% to 57%."

Source: "Critical Issues in Education," Georgia Alliance for Public Education, Fall 1990.

Fairness in Comparisons

The nation's commitment to educational equity has been accompanied by a growing emphasis on background characteristics of students and on contextual variables, such as poverty rates and school finance, distinguishing schools and districts. The achievement of similar outcomes in two schools may easily represent strikingly different levels of accomplishment on the part of students and school staff. Fairness in comparisons requires sensitive attention to the needs students bring to the school and to the resources the school can bring to bear on these needs. The panel rejects the notion that we should create one set of expectations for some students and a different set for others. Expectations need to be uniformly high and all students should be encouraged and helped to meet them. Few youngsters fail by themselves. Student failure represents a shared responsibility of the student, the family, the school, and the community. With respect to indicators, the panel's point is that students, schools, and districts face different problems; comparison indicators should not cavalierly ignore them.

Expectations need to be uniformly high and all students should be helped to meet them.

Burden

The information requirements of the federal government have little in common with those of the school superintendent or principal. Several indicator systems probably need development in order to respond to these diverse needs. Each of these systems will impose heavy costs in time and money, and can compete for the active cooperation of respondents.

Corruptibility of Indicators

When the stakes involved with an indicator system are high, involving perhaps financial rewards or state sanctions, the local pressure to produce the desired statistical outcomes is enormous. Evaluation procedures and measures can quite readily be altered in response to this pressure. For example, there have been reports of schools discouraging or preventing students likely to score poorly on examinations from taking required tests.

Problems Cannot Be Dismissed

These problems should not be dismissed or swept under the rug. The experience of the Department of Labor in developing the Consumer Price Index (CPI) illustrates what lies before the nation's educators. The CPI is not a trivial issue of concern largely to statisticians. Over one-quarter of a trillion dollars are indexed to this indicator with federal and state taxes, retirement funds, social security payments, and wage contracts dependent on its rise and fall. Work on the CPI began in the 1920s and 1930s and efforts to clarify the underlying conceptual basis of the CPI began seriously in the 1960s. But as recently as 1986, leading economists told Congress that major policies are being driven on the basis of statistical data badly in need of revision.[1] The panel is convinced that similar problems and difficulties lie before the nation's educators and analysts in fully developing education indicators.

There is every reason to believe these difficulties can be overcome. Considerable progress has been made in recent decades in improving measurement of school performance. Until the 1960s, federal education data collection was dominated by data on enrollments and graduation rates as measures of performance.[2] Since that time, a variety of efforts funded by the Departments of Education, Defense, and Labor have expanded the public's knowledge of what students know and how well American schools and colleges are performing. The nation's task is to build upon and extend that progress.

[1] Horn, Robin and Carolyn Winter, "Common Factors in the Development of Economic Indicators: Lessons Learned." Washington, D.C.: Decision Resources Group, May 1989.

[2] See Richard J. Murnane, "Improving Educational Indicators and Economic Indicators: The Same Problem," *Educational Evaluation and Policy Analysis*, Summer 1970.

Chapter 3

WHAT IS NEEDED

The task before the nation's policymakers and educators is the development of an education indicator system that can monitor and assess complex educational phenomena that may change frequently as public interests develop and shift. Under these circumstances, the information system must be capable of producing high quality data capable of meeting the demands the public and policymakers place on them. The challenge before this panel, NCES, and the education community is how to create such a system while respecting the complexity of the educational enterprise and making a start in tackling technical problems.

The critical first step is to define the conceptual framework that guides the development of the system.[3] The panel advances a three-part framework for the indicator information system it proposes—a set of fundamental beliefs about the value and purposes of the indicator system, a statement of the criteria that should shape its development, and six critical issues that define and give meaning to those criteria.

FUNDAMENTAL CONVICTIONS

An effective indicator information system must first be grounded in a new vision of how data can help us understand and improve the educational enterprise. That vision, in the panel's view, can be created around several fundamental principles.

Indicators should address enduring issues. We should assess what we think is important, not settle for what we can measure. Because of the technical nature of many of the questions surrounding

---

[3] See Janet L. Norwood, "Distinguished Lecture on Economics in Government: Data Quality and Public Policy," (Journal of Economic Perspectives, Vol. 4, Number 2, Spring 1990) for a discussion of the critical importance of conceptual frameworks in the Consumer Price Index, Producer Price Index, and measures of health care quality and of poverty.

education indicators—and the cost of new techniques and data collection—the first instinct is to develop an indicator system based on the information available and what we already know how to do. Such an approach will avail us little. We can already define the proportion of adults with high school diplomas or college degrees. We can roughly assess school support, student financial assistance, and student performance in selected areas. These are important achievements. But enduring issues require us to ask how well our school and college graduates are prepared to function in a changing economy, how effective our institutions are as places of learning, and how much students care to retain—and enlarge upon—what they have learned after their last examination is behind them.

The first instinct is to develop an indicator system based on the information available and what we already know how to do.

The public's understanding of education can be improved by high-quality, reliable indicators. The nation's students, parents, educators, employers, and public officials have to have much more reliable and accurate information about how well we are doing. We cannot improve education in the United States if we cannot identify and describe both its strengths and its weaknesses. At the same time, indicator information must be accessible to, and understandable by, the public. Much of the existing work on indicators and education data is restricted to analysts and professionals and, even when publicly available, is largely incomprehensible to the non-expert. The presentation of indicator information to the public must be improved.

The panel believes that an indicator system should not simply serve policymakers; it must also inform and improve public understanding. Indicators in the United States bear a particular burden. In France it used to be said that each day the Minister of Education knew what page of the text was open before every student. No comparable degree of centralization has ever existed in the United States. The American system of education is highly decentralized through 56 states and territories, about 15,000 school districts, and over 3,200 colleges and universities. In this decentralized system of governance, indicators must do more than simply *not misinform* the public. They must educate the public.

An effective indicator system must monitor education outcomes and processes wherever they occur. Virtually everyone agrees that learning and schooling are not synonymous. A high-quality system of indicators will explore learning in whatever context it occurs—in the home, in the family, in the community, on the job, in proprietary programs, as well as in schools and colleges. This principle is particularly important as education and training services are extended to non-traditional students.

An indicator system built solely around achievement tests will mislead the American people. Despite the panel's insistence that an effective system of indicators must assess learning, a system built solely around achievement is insufficient. As both the national education goals and AMERICA 2000 recognize, students will not learn more simply because we require them to take more tests. Students will learn more when schools are organized to engage them in challenging subject matter and the entire community unites behind learning. The practical implication of this conviction is that the indicator system must go beyond assessments of student performance to describe significant aspects of the educational environment, including curriculum, teacher quality, school organization, community support, and equity. These aspects of the educational enterprise are important in their own right and essential to learning. Ignoring them because they are often difficult to define or measure may defeat the effort to improve education before it is begun.

Students will not learn more simply because we require them to take more tests.

The panel also believes that traditional multiple-choice tests are inadequate measures of student achievement. Current definitions and measurements of achievement do not encourage genuine student effort; hence, these tests do not fully realize their potential to advance student learning. Indicators restricted to achievement as traditionally assessed impoverish our understanding of what teaching and learning are all about. Ultimately, they will impoverish the very students our schools and colleges are intended to serve (see box on following page).

An indicator system must respect the complexity of the educational process and the internal operations of schools and colleges. The panel is convinced that education indicators should not attempt to prop up the scientifically unsupportable view of education as nothing more than a special kind of "black box"—i.e., a mysterious process into which resources are poured and specific, and predictable, kinds of results emerge. Causality obviously exists in the educational system. Good teaching matters. Hard work by students makes a

difference. Stability in the home and the community is important. But
many of these factors are too subtle to be captured by today's
relatively primitive measuring tools.

**Higher education and the nation's schools can no longer be
permitted to go their separate ways.** Despite the symbiotic
relationship that has always characterized American schools on the
one hand, and the nation's colleges and universities on the other, each
has gone its own way in matters of assessment, monitoring, finance,
and public accountability. But the two share a common purpose:
developing the skills, talents, and competence of students. Moreover,
K-12 and higher education mutually depend on each other. Schools
rely on colleges and universities for the preparation of elementary and
secondary teachers. Higher education, in turn, is dependent on the

---

LIMITATIONS AND MISUSES OF STANDARDIZED ASSESSMENTS

Even the best of current efforts within NAEP only provide a view of children's
command of basic academic knowledge and skills in mathematics, reading, and
writing. While these competencies are important prerequisites for living in our
modern world and fundamental to general and continuing education, they represent
only a portion of the goals of elementary and secondary schooling. There are
major curriculum areas, such as the humanities, that have never been addressed by
NAEP. And then there are the aesthetic and moral aims of education that remain
beyond the purview of current assessment techniques.

The Academy Committee is concerned lest the narrowness of NAEP may have a
distorted impact on our schools. When test results become the arbiter of future
choices, a subtle shift occurs in which fallible and partial indicators of academic
achievement are transformed into major goals of schooling....

At root here is a fundamental dilemma. Those personal qualities that we hold dear
— resilience and courage in the face of stress, a sense of craft in our work, a
commitment to justice and caring in our social relationships, a dedication to
advancing the public good in our communal life — are exceedingly difficult to
assess. And so, unfortunately, we are apt to measure what we can, and eventually
come to value what is measured over what is left unmeasured. The shift is subtle,
and occurs gradually. It first invades our language and then slowly begins to
dominate our thinking. It is all around us, and we too are a part of it. In neither
academic nor popular discourse about schools does one find nowadays much
reference to the important human qualities noted above. The language of
academic achievement tests has become the primary rhetoric of schooling.

Source: Committee of the National Academy of Education, "Commentary on
*The Nation's Report Card: Improving the Assessment of Student
Achievement.* Report of a Study Group of the National Academy of
Education. Washington: National Academy of Education, 1987.

schools for the preparation of entering undergraduates. An effective indicator system should recognize these common interests and embrace both schools and colleges.

CRITERIA FOR AN INDICATOR INFORMATION SYSTEM

These principles point the way ahead. The panel believes that the nation needs an *education indicator system, organized around major policy issues, that is capable of shedding light on the educational process from many angles.* How can we define such a system? Three criteria appear essential:

- **Indicator information must focus first on what matters most about learning and about schools and colleges.** This is the kind of "bottom line" assessment that most members of the public expect. The panel believes the nation needs to create a system with a dual focus on both *learner outcomes* and the *quality of the nation's educating institutions. A* truly effective indicator system must forcefully and fully address student learning and examine the quality of the nation's schools and colleges.

- **Indicator information must assess the social context within which education takes place.** In most immediate terms, we need a much better understanding of the conditions of families with young children, and of *children's readiness* to learn as they enter the formal educational system. In more general terms, we need to know about *societal support for learning.* These two topics can be thought of as "leading indicators" that scan the educational environment. If the public is to understand not only educational performance but also the environment in which schools and colleges pursue their mission, it is essential that we have a much better understanding of such issues.

- **Indicator information must reflect important national values and aspirations for education.** Information about students, schools, colleges, and community support is important. But larger national values and aspirations lie beyond individual classrooms, lecture halls, and the immediate community. These include *educational equity* and the contributions that education makes to the nation's well-being, particularly to its *economic productivity. A* valid and reliable education indicator system must respond to these concerns.

These three criteria represent a major challenge. The panel does not advance them lightly. These criteria ask that the nation act on the understanding that a comprehensive indicator system, not a handful of key indicators, is required. They ask that the nation acknowledge that neither traditional indicators (e.g., years of schooling completed) nor traditional achievement tests alone can capture the full richness of

An effective indicator system must forcefully and fully address student learning and the quality of the nation's schools and colleges.

23

what needs to be assessed. They ask that we abandon the search for a few education indicators and proceed with the task of developing a comprehensive indicator system appropriate to education. The panel has every confidence that these criteria can be met if indicators are developed around enduring, significant educational issues.

SIX ISSUE AREAS

The panel believes an indicator information system organized around enduring educational issues can give life and meaning to these criteria. The panel suggests six issue areas as a place to start:

(1) Learner Outcomes: Acquisition of Knowledge, Skills, and Dispositions

(2) Quality of Educational Institutions

(3) Readiness for School

(4) Societal Support for Learning

(5) Education and Economic Productivity

(6) Equity: Resources, Demographics, and Students at Risk.

Figure 1 arrays these issue areas against the panel's three criteria.

Figure 1

Criteria and Issue Areas for a Comprehensive Indicator System

Indicator information must focus first on what matters most about learning and about schools and colleges.

(1) Learner Outcomes: Acquisition of Knowledge, Skills, and Dispositions

(2) Quality of Educational Institutions

Indicator information must assess the social context within which education takes place.

(3) Readiness for School

(4) Societal Support for Learning

Indicator information must reflect important national values and aspirations for education.

(5) Education and Economic Productivity

(6) Equity: Resources, Demographics, and Students at Risk

THE ISSUE AREAS AND THE EDUCATION GOALS

The six issue areas are consistent with but, in several important respects, go well beyond the goals chosen by the President and the governors in February 1990.

Perhaps the most important difference is the following: The panel explicitly wanted to broaden the vision incorporated in the national goals. Many of the concerns of interest to the panel are already included in the goals (e.g., the rights and responsibilities of citizenship and preparation for productive employment). But several major concerns (e.g., opportunity to learn and student engagement with subject matter) are not. In the panel's view, it is essential that an indicator system incorporate such topics; many important aspects of the educational enterprise are not goals in the sense of national policy outcomes but they are fundamental to effective education.

The panel wanted to broaden the vision incorporated in the national goals.

The goals, quite appropriately, treat education as an instrument of national policy. But schools and colleges are far more than agents of the state; in a free society they are the institutions through which adults realize their hopes for the next generation and young people explore their talents and develop their aspirations. The debate about education indicators, in short, must be recast to incorporate not only the instrumental policy aims of education but the imperative for schools and colleges to help all Americans live and learn their way through full and satisfying lives.

Despite this major difference, the panel's issue areas reflect every significant aspect of the national goals and, indeed, major elements of the President's education strategy, AMERICA 2000. The goals, in fact, helped stimulate the panel's thinking about the issue framework. The following paragraphs align the panel's six issue areas to the six goals.

Learner Outcomes encompasses much of Goal 3 (student achievement and citizenship), Goal 4 (science and mathematics), and Goal 5 (adult literacy, including exercising the rights and responsibilities of citizenship). The panel's issue area, however, is broader in conception, incorporating not simply demonstrated competence in a limited range of school subjects but, more broadly, the capabilities of our young people to live and work productively in a new century and a different economic age.

Education and learning are profoundly affected by what happens to children outside schools.

Quality of Educational Institutions includes, but goes well beyond, Goal 6 (safe, disciplined, and drug-free schools). The panel is convinced that although the goal is a significant policy issue, it is an inadequate definition of the kind of broad issue area that should serve in the development of indicators. Everyone supports the goal of safe, disciplined, and drug-free schools, but an indicator system should also try to capture the nature of schools as civilized institutions for both students and adults. Measurement problems may make it difficult to demonstrate conclusively that decent environments are related to student achievement. But schools should be humane institutions, and an indicators system should attend to this characteristic as worthy in its own right.

Readiness for School is directly analogous to Goal 1 (readiness for school).

Societal Support for Learning has no direct corollary among the goals, although it relates directly to the AMERICA 2000 strategy. This issue area represents a clear statement by the panel that education and learning are profoundly affected by what happens to children outside schools, during what AMERICA 2000 calls the "other 91%" of student time. An indicator system that ignores the family, communities, and public support (including financial support) for schools and colleges will be seriously flawed. The panel applauds the President and the Secretary of Education for acknowledging that attainment of the goals requires "communities in which learning can occur." This issue area promises to provide the information required to act on that part of the President's education strategy.

Education and Economic Productivity touches directly on Goal 2 (high school completion) and different aspects of several other goals. The panel believes that concerns such as international competitiveness, the skills of the college-bound and the non-college-bound, adult literacy, and labor supply-and-demand deserve focused attention in the indicator information system. This issue area offers the opportunity to provide that focus. It also responds to elements in several of the national goals (e.g., "preparation of students for productive employment in our modern economy"—Goal 3; and "every adult American will be literate [and able to] compete in a global economy"—Goal 5) related to productivity and economic competitiveness.

Equity represents one of this society's most important values, but none of the six national goals focuses exclusively on it. This issue area ties together several of the specific objectives within the national goals, including "all disadvantaged and disabled children will have access to high quality preschool programs," and "children will receive the nutrition and health care needed to arrive at school with healthy minds and bodies" (Goal 1); "the gap in high school graduation rates between American students from minority backgrounds and their nonminority peers will be eliminated" (Goal 2); "the [achievement] distribution of minority students...will more closely reflect the [achievement of] the student population as a whole" (Goal 3); "the number of...students, especially women and minorities, who complete degrees in mathematics, science, and engineering will increase significantly" (Goal 4); and "the proportion of those qualified students, especially minorities, who enter college; who complete at least two years; and who complete their degree programs will increase substantially" (Goal 5). The panel believes inclusion of this issue area within an indicator system is an essential signal to the public that the nation is seriously committed to equity in American education.

THE ISSUE AREAS IN BRIEF

The panel suggests its six issue areas as a starting point for national discussion and reflection about what matters in American education. They are offered as a set of basic ideas and priorities that should suffuse national thinking not just about indicators but about education in general. They reflect what is important in American education and, hence, what is important in monitoring the health of the enterprise.

Figure 2

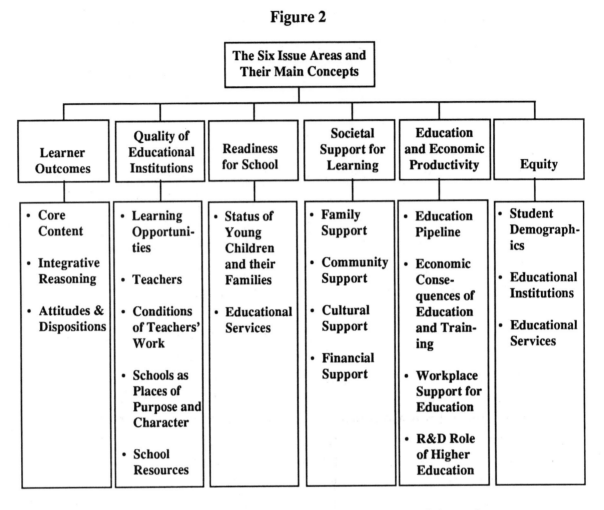

Part II of this document outlines, in detail, a structure of the major concepts and sub-concepts underlying each of these issue areas. Highlights of the discussion in Part II are summarized here and outlined in Figure 2, as a foundation for the recommendations presented in the next chapter.

What Matters Most: Students and Institutions

The panel is convinced that most members of the public expect that a credible indicator system will be able to monitor both what students know and are able to do, and how well the nation's schools and colleges are functioning. It should also be clear that the panel believes it would be a mistake to assess achievement alone or ignore the forces outside educational institutions that affect schools and schooling. That being said, we want to state clearly that achievement must be assessed and that external forces cannot be used to excuse poor institutional performance.

In taking up "what matters most" therefore, the panel believes two major issue areas are essential: learner outcomes and the quality of educational institutions.

Learner Outcomes: Acquisition of Knowledge, Skills, and Dispositions. No matter who raises the call for indicators to monitor the progress of American education, learning is the critical component. Interest in what students know and can do—how well prepared they are for life, work, and responsible citizenship—is intense.

The panel's conception of learner outcomes goes far beyond testing student achievement in a limited number of subjects. The panel includes the broad array of knowledge, skills, and attitudes that the larger society expects schools and colleges will help develop in young people. The guiding principle in this issue area can be found in the question: What do most parents hope education will do for their children? The answer is reasonably straightforward. Most parents expect that schools and colleges will help develop their youngsters into reasonably happy, competent young people, equipped with the ability to make a start in adult life. At high school and college commencement exercises every year, most parents hope for little more; and most are willing to settle for little less.

These hopes can be played out in different ways. Some young people seek further education—in colleges, trade schools, or in graduate or professional education. Others are interested largely in finding and holding a decent job. But whatever path they choose, young adults sooner or later have to find a place in their local community with all that that implies—getting along with others, considering whether or not to start a family, and assuming at least the minimal obligations of being a good neighbor and citizen.

The panel is convinced that many existing indicator development activities are too narrowly focused. The nation needs a much broader definition of appropriate learner outcomes and the panel suggests three

Achievement must be assessed; external forces cannot be used to excuse poor institutional performance.

major concepts to guide the development of indicators in this issue area: command of core content, integrative reasoning, and attitudes and dispositions.

- **Core Content:** This major concept covers the store of facts and knowledge grounded in traditional subject matter—English, mathematics, natural science, humanities and the social sciences, music and the other arts, and foreign languages.[4] The panel believes we need to know how much of this traditional knowledge students have accumulated and can use, and how they reason with this information within the context of each discipline, e.g., science or mathematics.

- **Integrative Reasoning:** This incorporates skills that cut across knowledge in specific fields. The critical component here is the faculty of integration, the ability to reason about, and apply insight to, complex issues, drawing on knowledge from distinct areas of core content. This major concept is particularly important to four complex areas of modern life: (1) workplace competence in managing and using resources, information, interpersonal skills and communication, technology, and systems; (2) science and technology; (3) international understanding; and (4) social diversity and cultural pluralism.

- **Attitudes and Dispositions:** This concept has to do with the human qualities that everyone hopes schools and colleges will nurture, including honesty, tolerance, a sense of community, self-directedness, teamwork and cooperative learning, commitment to craft, and attitudes toward learning—participation and engagement—that encourage students to stay in school and make the most of their time there.

With respect to assessing learner outcomes, the panel believes that policymakers should encourage the development of state-of-the-art assessment technologies for samples of students at the state and national levels. These technologies are capable of developing much greater insight into the skills and competence of young Americans (see box on following page).

Quality of Educational Institutions. Much of the public attention to institutional improvement in recent decades has focused on resources. Expenditures per pupil, the number of books in libraries, the availability of science laboratories, and distinct services for special student populations are, intuitively, important. At the postsecondary

---

[4] This subject matter reflects, but is not identical to, the basic competencies outlined in *Academic Preparation for College: What Students Need to be Able to Do*. New York: The College Board, 1983. As that document points out, conversations with business leaders confirmed that the core content described here is relevant for the college-bound, those in college, and those students leaving high school for the world of work.

NEW ASSESSMENT TECHNIQUES

In 1990 the Learning Research and Development Center and the National Center on Education and the Economy suggested the development of a sophisticated new national examination system that emphasizes alternative assessment techniques. An excerpt from that report follows:

"When fully developed, the National Examination System would include three forms of examination: performance examinations, portfolios, and projects. Students would sit for timed performance examinations, which would ask them to demonstrate that they have mastered the curriculum on which the examinations are based. Though these examinations might include some multiple choice questions, much of the examination would require self-generated and more elaborate responses. Portfolios would be assembled from work that a student did over a period of months or years, documenting the capacity to create a number of different work products and select the best of them. Projects would be used to give students an opportunity to demonstrate their capacity to apply what they know in the context of solving a complex problem over a period of time, often in association with others. All of these modes of assessment would stress the application of knowledge and skill in real life situations, situations in which there is rarely only one right answer to a problem and in which much of the art of solving the problems lies in framing it well. This combination of modes of assessment is designed to accommodate a variety of styles of learning and of demonstrating competence. These demonstrations of competence could occur over a period of years so that students need not feel that everything depends on what they do in a day or two of high pressure examination. They can begin to take pride, instead, in a record of cumulative achievement."

Source: "Setting a Standard: Toward an Examination System for the United States." Pittsburgh: LRDC, October, 1990.

---

level, the emphasis placed on institutional resources by accrediting agencies tends to reinforce this focus.

But these indicators hardly appear adequate to the task of defining institutional quality. In recent years, therefore, attention has turned to how schools and colleges actually function as organizations. The panel suggests five main concepts to guide indicator development:

- **Learning Opportunities:** Counting years of schooling—or days in a classroom or course credits as an undergraduate— is not an indicator of knowledge acquired. The nation needs much more sensitive barometers of institutional quality that also assess exposure to subject matter, the nature of learning activities, processes for assigning students within the school, and curricular integration. Much of what students do not "know" reflects what, in fact, they have never been taught (see box on following page).

ACHIEVEMENT AND CURRICULAR CONTENT

Some of the most compelling evidence about the relationship between achievement and curricular content comes from the Second International Mathematics Study (SIMS).... SIMS researchers...found real— and striking— differences between the ways curricula are organized in the highest-achieving countries and the way they are organized in the United States. At the lower-secondary level, the Japanese curriculum emphasizes algebra; the curricula in France and Belgium are dominated by geometry and fractions. In contrast, U.S. schools allocate their curricula more equally across a variety of topics — thus covering each subject much more superficially. The mathematics curriculum in U.S. schools is characterized by extensive repetition and review, and little intensity of coverage. This low-intensity coverage means that individual topics are treated in only a few class periods, and concepts and topics are quite fragmented.

Source: Lorraine McDonnell, et. al., *Discovering What Schools Really Teach.* Santa Monica: The RAND Corporation, June 1990.

- **Teachers:** Intelligent, competent, and committed people are central to every human enterprise. Relevant issues in this main concept cover teachers and instructors entering schools and colleges, professional preparation, and competence in the classroom.

- **Conditions of Teachers' Work:** The concept of teachers' work includes access to basic classroom resources and supporting resources taken for granted by professionals in other fields, influence over core matters of work such as textbook selection, and support for developing teachers' craft through sustained commitment to staff development.

- **Places of Purpose and Character:** Good schools are not corporate franchises—identically stamped out across the countryside. Each is individually shaped, even owned, by those who spend their time there—students, teachers, parents, and administrative staff. These are environments that daily sustain teachers in their work, engage students in their learning, and operate on the clear assumption that "here, in this building, everyone matters."

- **School Resources:** The concept of "school resources" refers to the adequacy of the resources available within the school itself. We believe that indicator data need to be developed around four sub-concepts: quality of buildings and facilities, library support, laboratories and technology available in the school, and the adequacy of professional support (counselors, librarians, and nurses) in the school.

Leading Indicators: Trends in Education

In the private sector, business leaders, economists, forecasters, and planners turn without hesitation to prominent "leading indicators" to anticipate how economic developments will affect their operations or those of their clients. Changes in indicators such as new business starts, construction permits, the prime rate, or orders for heavy equipment offer important clues about the strength or weakness of particular business sectors, both locally and nationally.

Education administrators at the local level often behave in much the same way. Groundbreaking for a major new housing development or apartment complex automatically prompts a school superintendent and local principals to think about whether the existing schools can absorb the children of large numbers of new families. The closing of major industrial plants employing thousands of workers prompts consideration of whether schools need to be consolidated as many families move elsewhere in search of employment.

The readiness goal is a powerful statement of national priorities.

But at the national level, policymakers rarely think broadly about developing indicators of leading changes that affect the educational enterprise. The panel believes an indicator system can help monitor important changes and suggests two issue areas with considerable promise: readiness for school and societal support for learning.

Readiness for School. Of the six issue areas identified by the panel, this is the one that most directly matches the national education goals.[5] The President and governors agreed in 1990 to the following goal for readiness: "By the year 2000, all children in America will start school ready to learn."

The panel considers this goal to be a powerful statement of national priorities. It is no secret that the world of childhood is changing. Many more children are growing up in single-parent families. One in four preschool children lives in poverty. The sharp increase in the number of working mothers and dual-career families means that child care and preschool have an increasingly critical role in children's early development.

The panel suggests two main concepts in the readiness area:

- **The status of young children and their families:** This includes the capabilities of children entering first grade, capabilities of 3-year-olds, and the health and family

---

[5] Although the panel did not pursue the suggestion, several members believed that the concept of "readiness" should be extended beyond readiness for elementary school to incorporate readiness for middle school, high school, or entry into college.

conditions of young children. In support of this concept, the panel considers it especially critical that profiles of the abilities of 3-year-olds and first graders (5- or 6-year-olds) be developed as part of a nationwide indicator system.

- **Educational services:** This concept refers to several aspects of teaching and learning in the early elementary grades as well as in kindergarten, preschool, and child care programs. It also extends beyond these institutions to encompass relationships with other service providers and with families.

"Societal support for learning" goes far beyond financial support.

Societal Support for Learning. Intentional education takes place not just inside schools and colleges, but within all of the institutions and situations where people live their lives—family and peer groups, churches, youth organizations, libraries and museums, the workplace, the military, the mass media, and the larger culture. The list of educating institutions in our society is unlimited.

There is a serious imbalance between the small amount of useful information we collect on non-school educative forces and the large amount we collect about formal educational programs. The imbalance has unfortunate effects, including a willingness to place unreasonable burdens on schools and a tendency to overlook the question of how family, community, and school can teach a consistent message about knowledge and values.

This issue area combines a number of traditional concerns about financial support of schools and colleges with issues that are relatively new to discussions of indicators, such as the amount of time parents give to schools and children's learning activities. At the broadest level, this issue area addresses contributions made by society and subgroups of society—the family, the individual, and corporations and other organizations outside schools—to education.

"Societal support for learning," therefore, goes far beyond financial support. It incorporates four major concepts:

- **Family Support for Learning:** This concept is concerned with the role of the family as educator and how the family supports learning. The panel advocates paying much more attention to specific values and to interactions between parents and children and between parents and the school.
- **Community Support:** Here the panel is interested in community support for learning and subject-centered programs, including mathematics, science, and the arts and humanities.

- **Cultural Support:** What is the cultural ethic surrounding American schools and colleges, the ethic within which they must operate and which helps shape young people's educational attitudes and behavior? What do polls and adult actions (voting behavior on school bond issues or reading patterns) reveal about societal support? How does the youth culture industry compete with education?
- **Financial Support from All Sources:** The panel calls for measures of financial effort and expenditure (for schools, colleges, and other education institutions) that emphasize readily understandable links with the allocation of resources for instruction.

Values and Aspirations

The people of the United States clearly expect the nation's schools and colleges to advance certain national values above and beyond the benefits education provides to individual students. National values and interests develop as national circumstances change. Before World War II, a system that provided high school diplomas to about 50 percent of the 18-year-old population and sent very few on to college comfortably met national expectations. Following the launching of Sputnik in 1957, national policy focused on improving mathematics and science instruction. Since at least 1965, the role of colleges and universities in advancing equal opportunity in the United States has been a stated national aim. Today, the nation's leaders call on education to provide a workforce equipped to help make the nation economically competitive.

The panel believes a comprehensive indicator information system should incorporate national values and aspirations and be broad enough to accommodate shifts in national priorities. Two issue areas appear to us to be promising: education and economic productivity, and equity in American education.

Education and Economic Productivity. Few phenomena have focused public attention on education as have the impact of technological change on the economy and the deterioration of the United States' international competitive position. Throughout this century Americans have relied on schools to help prepare youth for productive roles in the national economy and to extend the nation's prosperity.

35

Now considerable evidence suggests significant shifts in workplace requirements. Brainpower is replacing brawn. Work-site flexibility and problem-solving have become more important than standard routines designed by headquarters staff. According to many experts, our individual and collective well-being depends on the development of a workforce capable of thinking for a living.

The nation's well-being depends on a workforce capable of thinking for a living.

Employers also face challenges brought about by shifts in national demography. Decreased birth rates have produced a smaller pool of young workers than existed in the 1960s and 1970s. Complicating this picture is the fact that a larger share of these new job entrants are from groups who have not benefitted equally from formal schooling or historical hiring preferences—including minorities and those with language barriers.

The panel believes four main concepts form the foundation for a system of indicators on this topic:

- **The Education Pipeline:** What knowledge, skills, and dispositions will persons emerging from our educational institutions bring to the workplace in future years? Are sufficient numbers of youth acquiring the needed competencies at appropriate stages in their formal education?
- **Economic Consequences of Education and Training:** How does the economy utilize the skills and training of youth when they enter the job market and after? What types of education and training does the market value?
- **Workplace Support for Education:** What does the workplace do to train workers, to help youth and teachers understand the needs of the workplace, and to reinforce educational achievement?
- **Research and Development:** Beyond developing human capital, how are institutions of higher education encouraging economic growth through the discovery of knowledge and technological innovation?

The panel believes that a crucial missing piece of evidence in the area of education and economic productivity is a reliable assessment of the skills and competencies of young adults (aged 24-30). In the development of indicators in this issue area, this concern deserves a very high priority.

Equity—Resources, Demographics, and Students at Risk. The issue of equity cuts across all of the other issue areas outlined by the panel. In any of the other five, it is legitimate to ask, "How does this issue play itself out for different groups of students in different settings?"

The concern for educational equity is based on a fundamental belief in fairness. It transcends political boundaries and the narrow issues of interest groups. In American society, the values of fairness and justice are deeply held. When educational opportunities are unfairly distributed, we sense a problem, one of such significance as to demand attention and correction. Equity has become even more significant as the public has come to understand that the vitality of our society and economy depends upon attending to the educational needs of a large and growing minority population.

The issue of equity binds both student and institution.

An important task of the education system is providing equal opportunities for all, including early intervention to tackle the predictable problems that accompany some students, e.g., poor children, to school. Students experiencing difficulty in school can often be given "rapid remediation" so as to catch up.[6] In the longer term, some students' problems can be anticipated by early identification of "risk factors."

Equity as an issue frequently binds both student and institution. The educational problems of students from low-income families are widely discussed, if not fully understood. But few outside of education and the education policy community understand that low-income students attending schools with very high concentrations of low-income peers encounter a double disadvantage. First, they carry of the burden of living in poverty. Second, they attend schools in which many, even most, of their classmates are poor. In consequence, many of these students demonstrate achievement levels lower than would be predicted on the basis of the poverty of their own families alone. But the data available on high-poverty schools are very suspect. Most school districts define high-poverty schools by the proportion of

---

[6] See Joyce L. Epstein, "Effective Schools or Effective Students: Dealing with Diversity" in Ron J. Haskins and Duncan MacRae, Jr. (eds..), *Policies for America's Public Schools*. Norwood, N.J.: Ablex Publishing Co., 1988.

children receiving free or reduced-price lunches. But this definition does not fully reflect the incidence of family poverty since participation in the free-lunch program is voluntary.

The panel suggests three main concepts with respect to equity:

- **Demographic characteristics of students:** The nation needs regular reports on the basic demographics of students, including those in poverty, members of minority groups, children with physical and mental disabilities, children with limited English proficiency, and those attending schools with high concentrations of students from poverty backgrounds.

- **Characteristics of educational institutions:** How are students at risk distributed across levels of schooling (e.g., elementary, secondary, and postsecondary) and by public or private control? Where are these students located by state urban, suburban, and rural distributions?

- **Educational services:** Do students at risk enjoy access to the full range of educational opportunities? What kinds of services and learning opportunities are provided to at-risk students and how well-tailored are they to the needs of these youngsters?

The nation cannot recreate indicators in response to the latest headlines and educational fads.

Developing the Six Issue Areas

This structure of an education indicator information system is markedly different from most of the discussion of indicators that dominates public conversation today. It reflects the panel's belief that the complexity of education requires—requires absolutely—that indicators be grounded not solely in the instrumental ends of schooling or today's goals but in larger, enduring issues of teaching and learning. An effective indicator system should be focused not only on today's problems but also on tomorrow's and those that lie over the horizon. We will have many opportunities to refine and improve indicators; but the conceptual framework must, from the first day, be rich enough to incorporate the questions that will arise in the next generation. The nation cannot create and recreate indicators in response to the latest headlines and educational fads.

A great deal of work and several years of sustained effort will be required to make the indicator system proposed by the panel real. In each of the six issue areas, the major concepts and sub-concepts underlying the issue areas require development. For each of these, existing data and research have to be examined to determine if they are appropriate for indicator development or if new data or measures are required. Part II of this document reflects the panel's initial effort to think through the structure of information essential to each of the issue areas. But if such a system is to be created for nationwide indicators, federal data collection agencies will have to put forth a sustained effort. The following chapter suggests how that effort might be put in place.

Chapter 4

PUTTING THE SYSTEM IN PLACE

The panel believes that coming to terms with the indicator information requirements outlined in the preceding pages requires new ways of thinking about national data collection, information analysis, and public reporting. The recommendations that follow sketch the broad outlines of a vision of how the Department of Education's data collection activities can be transformed to help create a new indicator information system.

> ### I. THE PANEL RECOMMENDS THAT NCES VASTLY IMPROVE PUBLIC PRESENTATION OF INDICATOR INFORMATION

The National Center for Education Statistics (NCES) currently produces a useful compendium of indicators of elementary, secondary, and postsecondary education, *The Condition of Education*. When first developed as an indicators report in 1986, this document represented a major step forward in the public presentation of indicator information. But events have outstripped its utility as the flagship indicator report from NCES. Another major advance in reporting indicator information is essential.

I.1 NCES should develop biennial interpretive reports on each of the six issue areas defined by the panel.

The panel calls for a completely different kind of indicator report than NCES has been providing. NCES should produce a series of six analytical reports, one in each of the six issue areas identified by the panel. These documents should monitor progress in each issue area and serve as levers for educational change. If they are to meet that objective, it is essential that they appear in a timely fashion. The panel recommends, therefore, that each issue area be treated at least once every other year, i.e., NCES should organize itself to produce reports on three of the issue areas each year.

A different kind of indicator report is required.

The panel's view is that these new reports would go far beyond the kinds of indicator information now reported by the federal government. They should be based on many kinds of data, linked by thoughtful analytical commentary about what the data appear to mean, and how emerging research and case studies relate to major findings. In brief, although these reports should include numbers, charts, and tables, they should be far more than simply a quantitative assessment. Each of them should carry the message that single indicators, even with perfect measurement, cast a very narrow beam of light on a very large picture.

The panel believes these reports can be developed based on a conception of an "indicator pyramid"[7] (see Figure 3). At the very tip of the pyramid is the issue area itself, e.g., learner outcomes.

The left side of the pyramid corresponds to the conceptual levels (main concepts and sub-concepts) for each of the six issue areas. In the area of learner outcomes, for example, the panel proposes three main concepts—core content, integrative reasoning, and attitudes and dispositions. Moving down the left side of the indicator pyramid are sub-concepts referring to finer levels of detail. Using learner outcomes as the example once again, under the main concept of core content, the panel suggested several sub-concepts including English; mathematics; natural sciences; the humanities and social studies; music, art, and the performing arts; and foreign languages.

The right side of the pyramid represents indicator reporting levels. At the top, the panel places "key or composite indicators," framed with a broken line to note that, in the panel's opinion, such key indicators are not currently available. It may be possible, in the next several years, for NCES or other agencies to develop a set of such composite

---

[7] See Bryk, Anthony S. and Kim L. Hermanson, "Educational Indicator Systems: Observations on their Structure, Interpretation, and Use," (draft of a paper presented at a meeting of the Organization for Economic Cooperation and Development, Paris, France, November, 1990) for a preliminary description of an "information pyramid" which served as the prototype for the panel's indicator pyramid.

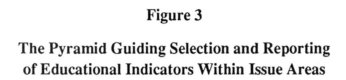

Figure 3

The Pyramid Guiding Selection and Reporting of Educational Indicators Within Issue Areas

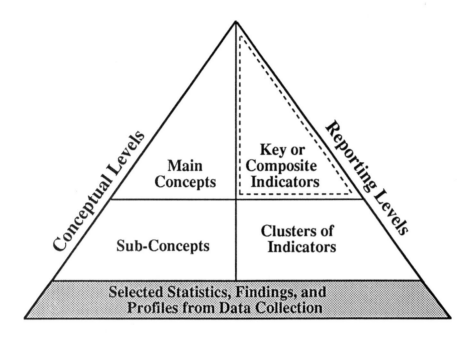

or key indicators for each of the six issue areas. But they are not available today.

Where then does the panel propose to provide indicators? We believe they can be created at the level below key or composite indicators. Moving down the right side of the pyramid, we place what the panel calls "clusters of indicators." These align completely with the sub-concepts on the left side of the pyramid. The panel believes that within the next few years it should be possible to agree on selected "clusters of indicators" corresponding to the main sub-concepts in each of the six issue areas. Take, for example the sub-concept of learner outcomes in mathematics. An indicator cluster on this topic might include:

- percentage of students scoring at the highest level in the NAEP mathematics test (level 350); the intermediate level (250); and the lowest level (150);

- the proportion of students in 8th and 9th grades who have

43

completed Algebra I, Geometry, or both;

- average scores on the College Board's mathematics achievement test and the proportion of high school juniors and seniors taking the test;
- average scores on the College Board's Advanced Placement test in mathematics and the proportion of high school students taking these tests;
- the proportion of college sophomores who have completed an introductory college-level course in mathematics;
- average scores on the quantitative section of the Graduate Record Examination for college seniors and the proportion of seniors taking this examination.

The list above simply illustrates the kinds of information that might be drawn upon to create clusters of indicators to more accurately reflect national performance in an essential sub-concept related to student achievement in mathematics. The panel has already noted that composite or key indicators are not now available but might, conceivably, be developed in the future. One way to develop such key indicators might be to closely analyze clusters of indicators over time. If a single indicator, over time, is found to be highly correlated with changes in the entire cluster, it is a likely candidate to serve as a key indicator for the entire sub-concept. A collection of such key indicators might possibly be developed to serve as its own cluster for main concepts.

Moving below the clusters, the entire pyramid (both the conceptual and reporting sides) is supported on a research base—statistics that offer a deeper understanding of the concepts being measured, along with research and data collection, case studies, program evaluations, and small-scale quantitative analyses bearing on the issue area in question. Conceptually, some of this is work at a very early stage of development. But the importance of this work in developing insights into each of the six issue areas is enormous.

I.2 NCES should also develop and publish interpretive reports that integrate information across issue areas on selected topics of pressing educational importance.

Assuming that recommendation I.1 is put in place, every 2 years NCES will publish six distinct, interpretive documents highlighting and analyzing major clusters of indicators in each of the issue areas:

learner outcomes, the quality of educational institutions, school readiness, societal support, education and the economy, and equity.

But even these six reports, useful as they are, cannot by themselves illuminate the inter-relationships of different concepts and subconcepts among the various issue areas. For example, the topic of national economic competitiveness cuts across the six issue areas: an analysis of youth's achievement in mathematics and science (learner outcomes) could be usefully integrated with student demographics (equity), student exposure to subject matter (quality of educational institutions), and academic research and development (education and economic productivity).

The possibilities for useful, informative work are endless; the point is that policymakers should exploit their access to a powerful, comprehensive, indicator information system by integrating disparate data sources across issue areas. The panel believes that reports such as these—presenting cross-issue-area linkages of major indicator clusters in a coherent analysis—promise to improve public understanding of education issues far beyond the insights provided by any single indicator, or cluster of indicators, standing alone.

Policymakers should exploit their access to a powerful, comprehensive, indicator information system.

I.3 NCES and the Department of Education should report meaningful, disaggregated data, including state-by-state comparisons, for each of the six issue areas.

Generalizations drawn from large data sets can easily conceal as much as they reveal. Data on average student performance or per student expenditures, for example, can easily conceal important differences in performance of, or expenditures on, students from different social or ethnic backgrounds or different geographical regions. Breaking large sets of data down by dimensions such as ethnicity or urban, rural, and suburban location is essential to obtaining a complete and accurate picture of the health of the education enterprise.

In this regard, analysts have made considerable progress in reporting state-by-state education data even though problems with the comparability of data and fairness persist. The panel endorses state-by-state comparisons of indicator clusters by major issue area. In this respect, the panel wishes to state that the "Wall Chart" has served its purpose, and served it well. When it was introduced, it was one of the few sources of information available to the public on the differences among states even though it lacked explanatory power. Since its initiation in 1984, it has been a spur for activity within individual states and for improving indicators—the Council of Chief State School Officers has initiated an indicator development project, the National Governors' Association is actively pursuing indicators to measure accomplishment of the nation's education goals, and NAEP is in the midst of gathering and publishing state-by-state assessment data.

Generalities can conceal as much as they reveal.

The panel believes that state-by-state data should be developed in each of the issue areas. In fact, the practical effect of this recommendation is to suggest that the Wall Chart be replaced with six wall charts, each focused on one of the panel's major issue areas.

> ## II. THE PANEL RECOMMENDS THAT NCES RETHINK ITS INTERNAL ORGANIZATIONAL ARRANGEMENTS SO AS TO ADVANCE THE INDICATOR INFORMATION AND REPORTING SYSTEM PUT FORWARD IN THIS REPORT.

The panel recognizes that NCES has greatly improved its capabilities to produce indicator information for the research community, policymakers, and the public while preserving the political neutrality that is essential to a statistical agency. But we sense that NCES has enjoyed much less success in realizing the analytic potential of the information it collects.

II.1 NCES should pay explicit attention to the relationship of its internal structure, organization, and management to the issue areas defined in this document.

In order to implement the recommendation in I above, it is essential that NCES's organizational structure reflect the new demands such a system will place upon it. Our hope is that these issue areas will reframe the discussion of education in the United States and the major government agency concerned with education data should lead the way.

Several possibilities exist for revitalizing NCES's organizational structure:

Strengthen the Agency's Analytical Capabilities. The panel believes that NCES should maintain and strengthen its capabilities to mount pilot studies and analytical investigations that support new indicator development.

Expand NCES's Substantive Capabilities. NCES employs substantive experts as well as statisticians primarily concerned with data quality and survey methodology. The panel believes that the agency needs to strengthen its substantive capabilities in each of the issue areas we have defined. Doing so will meet the dual need for data quality (as monitored most closely by experts in data collection) and data relevance (as monitored by substantive staff in each issue area).

NCES needs to strengthen its substantive capabilities in each of the issue areas.

The panel recommends that:

- NCES appoint a director for each issue area with a strong, substantive background in the specific area.
- The agency appoint a standing advisory panel of researchers and policy and practice clients (e.g., analysts, school teachers and administrators, public officials, and employers) to advise each issue area director about the substance of the issue area and presentation of each report. In the panel's view, each of these panels should initially be established for a 10-year period, with members appointed for revolving, periodic terms of between 3 and 5 years.
- NCES create an advisory panel of statisticians to review the data collection activities and data definitions used in each of its surveys. Each of the panel's issue areas will obviously draw on data from different surveys and studies. In consequence, it is essential that each of NCES's surveys employ compatible conceptual frameworks and data definitions.

The panel believes that these recommendations can go a long way toward ensuring that similar definitions are maintained across individual data sets; that opportunities for collecting indicator data across all of NCES's data bases are exploited; and that each issue area not only benefits from institutionalized substantive expertise but also communicates effectively with its intended audience.

> ### III. THE PANEL RECOMMENDS THAT THE SECRETARY OF EDUCATION AND THE CONGRESS PROVIDE ADEQUATE SUPPORT FOR NCES TO CONDUCT NEW AND REDIRECTED DATA COLLECTION ACTIVITIES.

As the panel wrestled with the the dimensions of the indicator system that it thought needed to be put in place, we recognized the enormous demands this system places on NCES and other government data collection agencies. But we were convinced that adding more poor data, and poorly-conceptualized data schemes, to what is already in place would leave the nation far short of a comprehensive indicator information system.

III.1 The Department of Education should seek, and Congress should approve, a major expansion in support for NCES and other federal agencies actively engaged in gathering information about educational institutions, children and young adults, and their families.

In the last decade, the American public has demonstrated an impressive appetite for more and more information about more and more aspects of American education. Collecting this information takes a great deal of time, requires a remarkable level of technical skill and ingenuity, and consumes large amounts of money. A reliable system of indicators cannot be created with the spare change and free time left over after "more basic" service needs have been met. The time has to be allotted and the money budgeted.

In talking about developing a system of "new indicators" the panel is really talking about developing the sensing and probing mechanisms by means of which our people and public officials can anticipate our educational future. Business activities in similar research and development and market exploration consume about 4 to 5 percent of corporate budgets. In the panel's view, if the public's demand for data and reliable indicators is to be met, public expenditures on data collection, analysis, and research, must increase several-fold.

Some of what we believe needs to be collected is already available in one form or another—from the School and Staffing Survey, from High School and Beyond and National Education Longitudinal Study (NELS:88) data, from the Elementary and Secondary and Higher Education Information Surveys (see box on following page). If the data we seek do not already exist, some of the information in these and other surveys can be readily adapted.

But this document clearly demands major new efforts to create new measures to assess students, to examine cognitive and affective domains that have not before been assessed, to test age groups that have not before been tested, and to gather data on institutions such as preschools, about which we have very little information. It is an intimidating agenda; but if the nation is serious about obtaining and analyzing better information about the condition of the nation's schools, colleges, and students, the agenda must be taken up.

Indicators cannot be created with spare change and free time.

In particular, the panel cites the following new information areas that require new work:

- **Learner Outcomes:** The panel's recommendations in this area call for a major new effort to develop and implement new assessment technologies in several areas—e.g., core subject matter, integrative reasoning, participation, and engagement with learning—with associated costs for sampling design and time-consuming assessment procedures.
- **Quality of Institutions:** The panel's recommendations in the area of school and college quality will require major new instrumentation efforts to gauge, among other things, learning opportunities, exposure to subject matter, assignment processes, and curricular integration.
- **A Profile of 3-Year-Olds:** The panel is proposing a significant effort to develop a profile of the nation's children. This will require major new work in assessment design and sampling and extremely expensive data collection, often requiring extended one-on-one interactions with children.
- **First Grade Assessment:** Like the 3-year-old profile, the first grade assessment (involving primarily 5- and 6-year-olds) will require extensive new pilot studies and a major implementation effort.
- **Young Adult Assessment:** The panel considers it essential, if we are to understand the educational and economic effects of educational programs, to expand into assessing the competencies of young adults (24-30-year-olds), a group including school dropouts and graduates, as well as college graduates.

SELECTED FEDERAL DATA SOURCES

The amount of data already available from the Federal government on education, children, and communities is immense. The following are some of the major sources:

U. S. DEPARTMENT OF EDUCATION

- *Common Core of Data Survey (CCD)*
- *Condition of Education*
- *Digest of Education Statistics*
- *Elementary and Secondary School Civil Rights Survey*
- *Federal-State Cooperative System for Public Library Data (FSCS)*
- *Financial Statistics of Institutions of Higher Education Survey*
- *High School and Beyond (HS&B)*
- *1987 High School Transcript Study*
- *Integrated Postsecondary Education Data System (IPEDS)*
- *International Assessment of Educational Progress (IAEP)*
- *National Adult Literacy Survey (NALS)*
- *National Assessment of Educational Progress (NAEP)*
- *National Household Education Survey*
- *National Education Longitudinal Study of 1988 (NELS, 88)*
- *National Longitudinal Study of the High School Class of 1972 (NLS-72)*
- *National Postsecondary Student Assistance Survey*
- *Private School Survey*
- *Projections of Education Statistics*
- *Schools and Staffing Survey (SASS)*
- *Statistics of Non-Public Elementary and Secondary Schools*
- *Statistics of Public Elementary and Secondary School Systems*
- *Statistics of State School Systems*

U.S. DEPARTMENT OF COMMERCE

- *Current Population Survey (CPS)*
- *Government Finances*
- *Regional Economic Information System*
- *State Personal Incomes*
- *Statistical Abstract of the United States*
- *Survey of Income and Program Participation*

U.S. DEPARTMENT OF HEALTH AND HUMAN SERVICES

- *Monthly Vital Statistics Report*
- *Vital Statistics of the United States*

National Institute of Mental Health

- *National Youth Survey*

U. S. DEPARTMENT OF JUSTICE

- *National Crime Survey*
- *National Youth Survey*

National Institute on Drug Abuse

- *National Household Survey of Drug Abuse*
- *Monitoring the Future: A Continuing Study of the Lifestyles and Values of Youth*

U.S. DEPARTMENT OF LABOR

- *Employment and Earnings*
- *Geographic Profile of Employment and Unemployment*
- *Handbook of Labor Statistics*
- *Special Labor Force Reports*

U.S. DEPARTMENT OF DEFENSE

- *Armed Services Vocational Aptitude Battery*
- *Population Representation Report*
- *Selected Manpower Statistics*

NATIONAL SCIENCE FOUNDATION

- *Longitudinal Study of American Youth*
- *Survey of Earned Doctorates*
- *Survey of Scientific and Engineering Expenditures at Universities and Colleges*

This list is by no means exhaustive. Clearly, NCES must develop priorities among these demands in consultation with experts; the point is that the agency cannot possibly respond to even the highest priority demands with the limited funds now at its disposal.

III.2 NCES should work with the National Governing Board of the National Assessment of Educational Progress to (1) expand the content areas in which NAEP data are currently collected and (2) test new measurement technologies within NAEP's ongoing assessment efforts.

The panel concurs with the line of reasoning developed by a committee of the National Academy of Education arguing that national assessments must be extended beyond reading, writing, mathematics, science, history, civics, and geography. All areas of the curriculum require attention and the nation can no longer afford to ignore the ability of students to apply their knowledge and skills across disciplines.

The panel encourages the NAEP board to continue to explore and incorporate new assessment methodologies into NAEP's ongoing work. For example, the 1990-91 reading assessment is more than a multiple-choice test: major portions of it are devoted to life-like assessments including writing, classroom observation, the use of portfolios, and asking students to comment on written material. Our hope is that NCES and NAEP will continue to expand and improve on these new "authentic" testing technologies.

III.3 NCES should intensify efforts to support both "longitudinal" studies that permit analysts to track the same age cohort over time, and "repeated cross-sections" that permit analysts to examine trends affecting specific age groups.

As a general recommendation about future measurement emphases, the panel believes strongly that more data need to be gathered—on students, institutions, funding, and the surrounding community—that permit the analysis of trends in such areas as achievement, financial support, attitudes, and shifting demographic characteristics. It is critical that the nation develop the capability to monitor educational change over time.

A sound indicator system should provide a motion picture of educational progress.

In this regard, we want to point out that no matter how valuable a specific, even large-scale, one-time, data collection activity may be, it represents simply a snapshot of students and institutions at a particular point in time. Snapshots have their uses; but a sound indicator system will also provide the nation with a motion picture of its progress. Longitudinal and cross-sectional data collection efforts help create these movies.

Longitudinal studies track the same cohort of students over time. If policymakers wish to understand what happens to young people as they move through the education system and into the world of work, data collection efforts have to identify these young people as early as possible and follow them for as long as they can. The panel believes that longitudinal studies starting with children as early as the age of 3 and following them through young adulthood should be a goal of NCES.

The value of longitudinal studies lies in three areas: First, they can be used to explore important transitions in students' lives. As students progress through the education system and make the transition into the adult world, the indicators that capture this process must have data that follow the progress of individuals over time. Policymakers' understanding of who drops out of school compared with who persists and who returns—in both secondary and postsecondary institutions— has been shaped significantly by two NCES longitudinal studies, the 1972 National Longitudinal Study of high school seniors and the 1980 High School and Beyond study of high school sophomores and seniors. Second, longitudinal studies provide the research base for testing the assumptions of existing indicators and developing models for new indicators. For example, most researchers today believe that the effect of school-level policies and practices on learning is revealed only through longitudinal measures of student achievement. Third, data that follow students and schools over time allow analysts to refine their understanding of what a particular indicator says and how well it is working.

At the same time, what analysts call "repeated cross-sections" are required if we are to understand and appreciate significant changes over time in educational issues or in specific populations (see box). Here, policymakers might want to answer the following kind of question:

- In the last 10 years, has the proportion of preschoolers living with only one parent gone up or down, and if so by how much?

- How has access to postsecondary education for minority Americans changed in the past 5 years?

NATIONAL ASSESSMENT: THE VALUE OF COMPARISONS OVER TIME

Findings from recent NAEP assessments provide evidence of progress in students' academic achievement. Results from the 1984 and 1986 assessments indicate that, on the average, students' proficiency in reading has improved across time, and proficiency in writing, mathematics, and science has improved in recent assessments after earlier declines. In addition, there is evidence that some strides have been made toward equity: Gaps in average academic performance that have historically existed between black students and their white peers and between Hispanic students and their white peers have been reduced by a considerable margin in some subjects.

Despite these positive signs, the remaining challenges are many. Not all ground lost during the 1970s and early 1980s has been regained, and there was considerable concern even at the time of the first assessments about the quality of student learning. In addition, a closer examination of the NAEP data indicates that recent gains in student performance have occurred primarily at the lower levels of achievement. For example, students have improved in their ability to do simple computation, comprehend simple text, and exhibit knowledge of everyday science facts. However, too few students develop the capacity to use the knowledge and skills they acquire in school for thoughtful or innovative purposes. And too few students learn to reason effectively about information from the subjects they study...

Overall, the NAEP data suggest that American education is at a crossroads. While academic achievement appears to be improving after years of decline, the continuing lack of growth in higher-level skills suggests that more fundamental changes in curriculum and instruction may be needed in order to produce more substantive improvements. The education system in this country needs to extend its focus from the teaching and learning of skills and content to include an emphasis on the purposeful use of skills and knowledge.

Source: Applebee, Arthur N. and Judith A. Langer and Ina V.S. Mullis, *Crossroads in American Education*. Princeton: Educational Testing Service, February 1989.

- How are student course-taking patterns in secondary school and undergraduate programs changing?
- Is student achievement in 8th-grade English, foreign languages, or mathematics going up or down.
- How much time are junior high school students spending watching television, or working, compared to 10 years ago— and which groups of students spend the most time in these activities?

IV. NCES SHOULD EXPAND ITS EXTERNAL EFFORTS TO (1) STRENGTHEN THE AGENCY'S NATIONAL LEADERSHIP ROLE IN DATA COLLECTION; (2) PROVIDE TECHNICAL ASSISTANCE TO STATES; AND (3) IMPROVE CAPABILITIES TO COLLECT INTERNATIONAL DATA.

Since a federal education agency was first created in 1867, the collection of education data and statistics has been seen as its critical role. The panel believes that NCES has a long and honorable tradition of meeting that obligation responsibly and well. But now, new challenges requiring new responses are placed before this agency. The panel has already outlined the new areas and kinds of measurements it believes NCES needs to address. We have commented on the need for NCES's organizational structure to reflect enduring educational issues. But our concern with the federal role extends beyond issues of data and management. It is directed toward the very mission of the agency itself.

To develop the indicator information system proposed in this document NCES must enlarge its leadership responsibilities in education data collection. What we are proposing is not the addition of a few new data items to the information agenda that is already in place. We are proposing a transformation of NCES's understanding of its own responsibilities in data collection, reporting, and the role of data and information in American education. The panel believes that NCES must build on existing efforts to provide leadership in data collection, provide technical assistance to states, and cooperate in developing first-rate international data.

IV.1 NCES should continue to assert a leadership role in defining national data standards.

Through the development of handbooks, manuals, and other products, NCES has sought to establish the basic conceptual structures, data categories, and definitions to be used in collecting and reporting education data. NCES should continue this important function and use this work to ensure that consistent standards are employed across data sets by federal and state agencies responsible for education statistics, and that opportunities for collecting indicator data across multiple data bases are fully exploited.

IV.2 NCES should improve its ability to provide technical assistance to states.

An important aspect of this leadership role is providing assistance to states, and to state systems, as they attempt to grapple with their own indicator development needs. The panel supports state-by-state comparisons where feasible and appropriate. But states, and state systems such as the Council of Chief State School Officers and the National Governors' Association, are actively engaged in indicator development programs of their own. NCES's mandate should be broad enough to encompass providing conceptual support, technical assistance, and expert advice to these efforts. In this regard, NCES's leadership in establishing a National Forum on Education Statistics to bring together federal, state, and regional experts to discuss data needs is exemplary.

The panel endorses the concept of a "mixed model" of education indicators.[8] This model envisions national indicators on the one hand, and state and local indicators on the other, with a subset of indicators held in common. At the national level, indicators developed from ongoing federal data collection activities would be specified, defined, and collected around national issues. Indicators in common would be collected independently by states using identical state/federal definitions and measures. State and local indicators would be specified, defined, and collected independently by states and local districts for their own use.

A "mixed model" of indicators— national indicators, state and local indicators, and a subset of indicators held in common.

---

[8] Jeannie Oakes, *Educational Indicators: A Guide for Policymakers.* Rutgers: Center for Policy Research in Education, October 1986.

International data: the ultimate benchmarks of educational performance.

One powerful tool at NCES's disposal in assisting states is the opportunity to permit states to "buy in" to major NCES surveys with supplementary samples of their own. This is an especially useful tool in states that have an indicator model in which they are interested but lack funds or expertise to develop appropriate instrumentation. These opportunities potentially strengthen NCES's own data collection activities. More to the point from the states' view, it permits individual states to employ data collection systems, methodologies, and instruments linked to national state-of-the-art efforts. Hence, NCES can advance important national interests: encouraging states to develop strong instrumentation in data collection areas of interest to them and to benchmark their own results with those of other states and the nation.

IV.3 NCES should expand its work with statistical agencies and institutions in other nations to cooperate in collecting international education data.

International data, properly collected and understood, may well be the ultimate benchmarks of educational performance and the most powerful data for understanding how well American schools, colleges, and students are performing.

NCES has been the lead federal agency working with international bodies developing indicator information. The panel supports these efforts and urges NCES to continue its collaborative activities with such groups as the Organization for Economic Cooperation and Development (OECD) and the International Association for the Evaluation of Educational Achievement (IEA).

A FINAL COMMENT

In the information age we face the paradox of having more and more data and less and less certainty about what they mean. Data never add up to knowledge without careful thought and they can never be reduced to wisdom through the expedient of creating a handful of indicators. The panel has argued that a carefully thought out education indicator information system can help the nation develop some wisdom about its educational problems and possibilities. But it can do so only if our people and our policymakers never lose sight of the human ends of education and the social nature of the institutions through which those ends are pursued.

This realization carries with it a set of corollaries for the education indicator information system. First, schools are pluralistic institutions. The information developed about them must be pluralistic in origin and serve many audiences. Second, the integrity of data collection and analysis must be protected from political intrusion. Governments change and presidents, cabinet officials, and members of Congress often decide to strike out in new directions. The public interest in education indicators can be protected from short-term partisan agendas only if the agencies collecting and analyzing information are supported in their efforts to develop comprehensive systems capable of responding to most major requests for information.

Finally, an indicator system should recognize that because education counts in the United States, data collection and analysis are fundamental public trusts for the citizens of today and tomorrow. Public trusts require prudent judgments in the development of education indicators. The challenge is to look over the horizon to see what educational issues may confront us in the future. An indicator system responding faithfully to that challenge will serve the public long and well.

Data can never be reduced to wisdom through the expedient of creating a handful of indicators.

PART II

AN INDICATOR SYSTEM TO MONITOR
THE NATION'S EDUCATIONAL HEALTH

SIX ISSUE AREAS TO MONITOR
THE NATION'S EDUCATIONAL HEALTH

In Part I of this document, the panel explored the need for a comprehensive education indicator information system, outlined six issue areas to guide the development of such a system, and proposed a new vision of indicator reports, organized by issue area, to improve public reporting of indicator information.

Throughout most of their tenure, members of the panel struggled with the intellectually demanding task of how to organize the major themes and priorities of the issue areas so as to capture the essential elements within each of them. The results of these efforts were summarized in Chapter 3.

Part II of this report develops the panel's thinking about the six issue areas. For each of the six, Part II expands upon the concepts and sub-concepts summarized in Chapter 3; touches on broad concerns where better indicator information can shed some light; points to existing data that promise to provide indicator information; and highlights data and information gaps.

This more detailed roadmap of the six issue areas is presented in the three chapters that make up Part II. Each chapter that follows is devoted to the issue areas associated with the panel's three criteria for an indicator information system. This roadmap is offered not as the final word on how these issue areas should be organized. Rather, it represents the panel's initial reflections on the enduring concepts and ideas that are essential to informed public discussion of American education. Seen in that light, these concepts and ideas should be the basic underpinnings of any indicator information system; they are offered as a starting point for national discussion, as a guide to thought, and as an invitation to all who care about the nation's educational future to join in this discussion.

Chapter 5

WHAT MATTERS MOST: STUDENTS AND INSTITUTIONS

As noted in Chapter 3, most members of the public expect a credible indicator system to monitor both what students know and are able to do, and how well the nation's schools and colleges are functioning. In taking up "what matters most" therefore, the panel believes two major issue areas are essential: learner outcomes and the quality of educational institutions.

LEARNER OUTCOMES: KNOWLEDGE, SKILLS, AND DISPOSITIONS

Measuring a relatively narrow band of knowledge and skills through grade 12 has occupied educational researchers, practitioners, and policymakers for most of this century. Educational achievement is seen as kind of a bottom line and is often regarded as the ultimate proof of whether the education system is performing satisfactorily. Measuring achievement in postsecondary education, particularly through graduate and professional school admissions testing, has also expanded in the last generation, but until recently it has received little comparable attention from the public or policymakers.

The panel is convinced that the nation needs a much broader definition of appropriate learner outcomes and suggests three major concepts to guide an indicator system in this issue area: command of core content, integrative reasoning, and attitudes and dispositions (see Figure 4 on following page).

Command of Core Content

The first order of business is the assessment of students' grasp of essential discipline-based knowledge, e.g., literature or mathematics. This major concept encompasses the store of facts and conceptual and procedural knowledge grounded in subject matter that the student can accumulate and use.

Figure 4

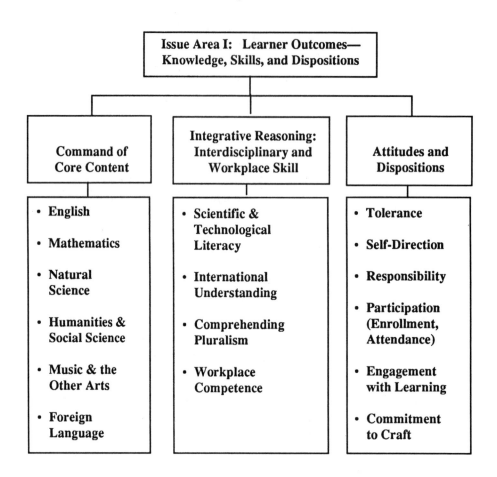

Six sub-concepts capture the main indicator areas of interest:

- **English:** Command of the English language is essential to life and work in the United States. The importance of skilled use of English—reading, writing, speaking, and listening cannot be overstated.

- **Mathematics:** Mathematics is the language of science, technology, business, and finance. All young people deserve to leave school proficient in performing both basic and complex mathematical operations and using quantitative reasoning to solve problems.

- **Natural Sciences.** As the use of technology accelerates in our national life, most people need some grasp of the concepts and processes of science. Here the panel is interested in the ability to think, reason, and solve problems through inquiry and investigation, drawing on important ideas and interrelationships in the life, earth, and physical sciences.

- **Humanities and the Social Sciences.** Young people need some understanding of the great developments, events, people, and literature that have created the world we know. Amidst the complexities of modern life, they also need to be familiar with the structure and functioning of political, social, and economic institutions.

- **Music, Art, and the Performing Arts.** The omission of music and the other arts from most reform rhetoric is a disappointing sign of the poverty of the public discussion about school improvement. The nation needs a much better understanding of how the expression of ideas and emotions through the arts develops aesthetic appreciation and encourages creative thinking, self-esteem, and motivation to learn.

- **Foreign Languages:** Knowledge of another language provides greater insight into the workings of one's own language and fosters greater awareness of cultural diversity among the peoples of the world.

Integrative Reasoning: Interdisciplinary and Workplace Skill

The second major concept in this issue area incorporates skills that cut across knowledge in specific fields. The critical component here is the faculty of integration. Students should be able to demonstrate command of the ability to apply reasoning and insight to complex issues, drawing as necessary on knowledge and information from distinct areas of core content.

Integrative reasoning is essential in modern life and today's workplace. It represents not the ability to recall bits and pieces of information but the "things" one can demonstrate one can do. These include communication, using technology and information effectively, and proficiency in working in a problem-solving capacity either alone or in teams. The Department of Labor's Secretary's Commission on Achieving Necessary Skills (SCANS) is in the midst of an effort to define and assess five key areas of workplace competence that represent one useful way of thinking about integrative reasoning on the job: Skilled workers, SCANS has concluded, demonstrate competence in managing and using resources, information, technology, interpersonal skills, and complex systems. Graduate students and faculty members are not the only people required to use knowledge in all of its complexity. Assembly-line workers, technicians, business owners, and supervisors have to draw on diverse disciplinary knowledge to get to the root of the complex problems technology today places in their path.

Quite apart from the world of work, the panel believes that education should enable students to apply their knowledge in an integrated way to the problems of the modern world. Three areas are particularly significant:

Scientific and Technological Literacy. Knowledge and understanding of scientific principles and phenomena are educational benchmarks in the information age. Our students and our people need to be able to apply scientific and technological knowledge to real problems—pesticide use, environmental warming, waste disposal, space exploration—and weigh the implications of alternative solutions to these problems.

International Understanding. As the world around us changes, it is essential that our people comprehend the importance of international interdependence, cultural differences, the possibilities for conflict, and economic and geographic influences on the nations of the world. Questions about comparative economic systems, why different cultures function as they do, and facility with other languages are central to reasoning in this cross-disciplinary area.

Comprehending Pluralism. As the United States becomes a more diverse society, our people will have to grapple increasingly with the reality of ethnic diversity, cultural differences, and the economic and social interdependence of people from many lands and cultures. The health of a complex interplay of cultural influences in defining and resolving national issues will be the hallmark of the health of the nation in the future.

Attitudes and Dispositions

The key question in this main concept has to do with the human qualities everyone hopes schools and colleges will nurture. These include participation and engagement with learning, and attitudes and dispositions about life and learning that were once summed up in the term "civic virtue"—honesty, tolerance, a sense of community, self-directedness, and a belief that effort expended today will be rewarded tomorrow.

American society hopes that youth will acquire a set of attitudes and dispositions over the course of their formative years. Many employers, for example, place great emphasis on employees' attitudes when asked to list qualities they seek in new workers. High on the agenda: adaptability, initiative, responsibility, commitment to craft, and pride in work. In the larger society, tolerance for diversity, a measure of concern for fellow human beings, the responsible exercise of citizenship, and a sense of social responsibility are essential to the functioning of local communities and the nation itself.

Attitudes toward learning constitute a significant portion of this concept. Indicators that fall under what the panel calls participation and engagement are both means and ends of the educational process. They not only facilitate the attainment of desired ultimate goals, they are themselves qualities that schools should cultivate.

We have few sources of information on what college seniors know and are able to do.

- **Participation:** This involves the choices students make—enrollment, attending classes, staying in school—that keep open the broadest array of educational and career options for the longest possible time.
- **Engagement:** How involved are high school and college students in their learning? Do they seek academically rigorous courses or are they satisfied to slide by with the minimum? This area encompasses student effort to take advantage of opportunities as well as how students use such resources as libraries.

Learner Outcomes for Postsecondary Students

Relative to education from kindergarten through grade 12, postsecondary education has been largely ignored with regard to systematic national assessment of students' skills and proficiencies. Recently, regional accrediting agencies, state legislatures, state boards of higher education, and Congress have called on institutions to document the performance of their students. One particularly visible instance occurred in 1989 when Congress insisted that colleges and universities publish graduation data of students engaged in intercollegiate athletics. In several instances new demands such as these have been met by resistance on the part of faculty or administrators.

With the exception of a few examinations for graduate and professional study (e.g., the subject area tests of the Graduate Record Examination) we have few sources of information on what college seniors know and are able to do. Certainly the data in this area are not nearly comparable to those available on elementary and secondary school students.

Implications for Indicators

The National Commission on Testing and Public Policy estimated in 1990 that between $700 and $900 million is spent annually on testing what students know. The federal government directly or indirectly sponsors a number of tests including the National Assessment of Educational Progress, the Armed Services Vocational Aptitude Battery, international assessments, and program evaluations for a variety of federal education efforts such as Chapter 1 of the Elementary and Secondary Education Act.

Unmet Needs. Despite this abundance of testing, the panel's principal concern is that many desirable outcomes of the learning process are not assessed in any significant way beyond the level of the individual school. NAEP does not assess many of the issues of concern to this panel, e.g., foreign language proficiency or employability skills. The panel is not aware of any statewide or national effort to assess integrative reasoning or the affective domain.

The panel also wants to point out with respect to attitudes and dispositions that the idea of measuring some of these outcomes necessarily confronts measurement problems as well as concerns about invasion of privacy. These represent very real difficulties. But the panel is convinced that in this society what is measured is what is valued. If we value the role of schools and colleges in developing the attitudes and dispositions of our young people, the effort to assess their success must be made.

NAEP's Contribution. In light of these difficult problems, it is important to understand what is currently available and how useful it is. A great deal of effort, for example, has been put into external reviews of NAEP in recent years. By and large, most of these reviews have endorsed the general concept of NAEP as an essential source of achievement information, in part because it is the longest standing effort and offers the promise of providing the most comprehensive, accurate, and useful data. NAEP, by itself, can provide the following:

- reading and mathematics assessments at least every 2 years starting in 1990;
- science and writing, at least every 4 years (writing was assessed in 1988 and science in 1990);
- history and geography at least every 6 years;
- a subject matter design that provides scale scores indicating the percentage of students who operate at different levels of proficiency within that subject and across age and grade groups;
- a "spiraling" sampling design that minimizes the number of items any one student has to respond to while producing considerable information across a range of items within each subject;
- performance measures from students at the transition points of 4th, 8th, and 12th grades; and
- racial/ethnic breakdowns at ages 9, 13, and 17 indicating differential performance between majority and minority Americans and the extent to which gaps in performance are closing over time.

The panel has to stress that there remains a need for multiple, pluralistic measures of student outcomes. NAEP, longitudinal surveys, international achievement surveys, and surveys of adult literacy and of attitudes of American youth must be maintained, in some cases developed. Moreover, the existence of state achievement results, national college entrance examination tests, military recruitment examinations, and even improved versions of nationally standardized achievement tests can serve as important crosschecks of the accuracy of individual measures of learning.

Traditional Achievement Tests. The panel wants to point out that most national assessments rely heavily on multiple-choice formats. Obviously, such tests have their uses. However, education and learning are complicated endeavors, and the panel believes the effort to assess the results must be equal to the task. "Authentic," "alternative," and "performance" are all terms applied to emerging assessment techniques. Whatever name they go by, their common denominator is that they call on students to apply their thinking and reasoning skills to generate often-elaborate responses to the problems put before them.

In many of these testing situations, there are multiple "correct" answers; in almost none of them is the student forced to select from a list of pre-specified multiple-choice alternatives. Extended writing assignments, hands-on science assessments, student portfolios, and group projects over time are the next generation of tests that will assess a new generation of Americans.

For NCES, these new techniques pose a challenging policy issue: How should these new testing technologies be blended into ongoing assessment and data collection efforts? The panel believes that these state-of-the-art testing technologies should be encouraged for sample student assessments at the state and national levels. The panel is convinced that such assessments can develop much richer insights into the skills and competence of American youth.

Data Burden. Undoubtedly, many of the panel's proposals for new measurement will be difficult to implement and their additional burden on institutions and students may encourage some resistance. If it is concluded that the panel's recommendations add too much to a system that is already overburdened, the panel recommends major revisions in the scope of current assessments. Clearly, if resources remain constant and current assessment requirements remain in place, federal officials will need to confront trade-offs between expanding the current system and modifying it to accommodate the panel's recommendations. Some existing assessments may need to be abandoned (e.g., specific mandated program evaluations). In the panel's view, however, failure to rework the system will continue to expose the nation to the risks of a mediocre indicator system that emphasizes fragments of knowledge that do not build to a meaningful whole.

QUALITY OF EDUCATIONAL INSTITUTIONS

In Chapter 3, the panel suggested five major concepts to undergird an understanding of the quality of educational institutions: learning opportunities, teachers, conditions of teachers' work, schools as places of purpose and character, and school resources (see Figure 5 on following page).

Figure 5

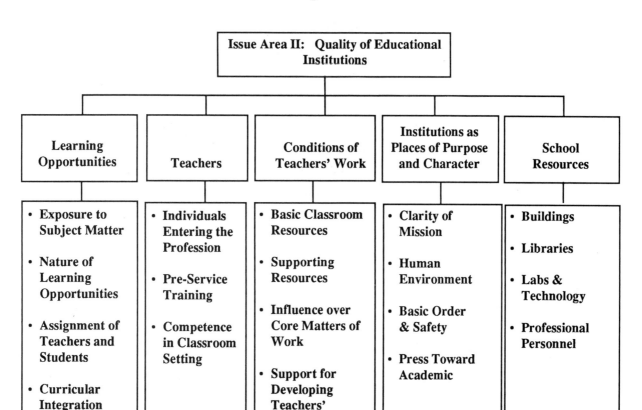

Learning Opportunities

Counting years of schooling—or days in a classroom or course credits as an undergraduate—is not an indicator of knowledge acquired. The nation urgently needs much more sensitive barometers of institutional quality that also assess exposure to subject matter, the nature of learning activities, processes for assigning students within the school, and the extent of curricular integration.

Exposure to Subject Matter. The panel believes that detailed information is needed on the actual subject matter to which students are exposed. Much of what American students "do not know" reflects, in fact, what they have never been taught. Indicators of exposure to knowledge need to be developed that line up with the content areas described in the preceding issue area.

We need to know: What kinds of learning opportunities are provided to different students in different schools? How much time is allocated to each subject, and what topics constitute the curriculum in each major area? Are texts available to all students, and, if so, how current are they and how much material is actually covered?

Counting years of schooling or undergraduate course credits is not an indicator of knowledge acquired.

Nature of Learning Opportunities. A major criticism of contemporary schools is that is that they encourage passivity in learning. Like adult "couch potatoes," students are expected to absorb, inertly, whatever modest amount of information is placed before them. Learning becomes not the development of skill in thinking and solving problems, but a numbing process of acquiring apparently unrelated facts, rules, and procedures.

Here the key questions become: What kinds of learning *activities* do students experience? Is science taught as basic facts and laws or as an area of human inquiry in which evidence and intuition combine to create new knowledge? Do students see mathematics as rote learning of formulae, or are they exposed to deeper understandings of mathematical phenomena? Is history a set of dates to be memorized or the story of the long march of human striving, conflict, and progress?

These issues are important because researchers are beginning to document, based on findings from IEA, NELS:88, and NAEP, that learning opportunities differ significantly in different schools. NAEP's 1991 results indicate, for example, that some middle-school mathematics teachers emphasize rudimentary arithmetic calculations and drills. In others, students are already working on algebra and elementary functions. In light of this information, the results are hardly surprising: The second group of students demonstrates far superior results in mathematics.

Assignment Processes. The organization of life in schools, colleges, and universities has become quite complex. Curricula have expanded; the professional staff has become more specialized; new services have been created to meet the needs of individual students. The assignment processes linking students to teachers to subject matter are a central feature of how schools work.

The panel believes that policymakers need to know: Are students encouraged to take challenging and demanding courses? Does the school maintain high expectations for all students, or simply for selected students? How are determinations made about assigning students to courses of varying levels of difficulty? What about teachers—how are they assigned to different classes and, in particular, how are they assigned among different schools within the same system? Finally, what do both students and teachers think about the assignment processes? Do they consider them fair and reasonable, or arbitrary and capricious?

Curricular Integration. Specific subject matter is important. But so is curricular integration. Adults are presented with very few complicated problems in life that can be attacked with the tools and techniques of a single discipline. In order to understand measures of integrative thinking developed under Learner Outcomes, we need to know how the curriculum is structured to encourage cross-disciplinary work and what student experience is in this regard. The significance of these questions is all the more important in higher education, where traditional concepts of liberal education have eroded and institutions are struggling to create a new sense of common purpose in undergraduate studies.

Adults are presented with very few complicated problems that can be attacked with the tools of a single discipline.

Teachers

Intelligent, competent, and committed people are central to every human enterprise. Relevant issues in this main concept cover teachers entering the profession, professional preparation, and the competence teachers demonstrate in the classroom.

Individuals Entering the Profession. The first focus is the academic preparation of those entering teaching. Which high school graduates are drawn into undergraduate teacher preparation programs? On nationally recognized tests of literacy, aptitude, or achievement, how do they compare with other undergraduates? For those entering the profession in mid-career, what is their academic background and work experience?

Pre-Service Training. The second sub-concept covers the experience of individuals in teacher preparation programs, the level of professional knowledge they demonstrate, and the practical experiences to which they are exposed. The preparation of teachers is too important to be satisfied with a simple cataloging of academic credits earned. We need to know what these students have done as undergraduates, what they have learned, and the nature of the practical experience they have received to prepare them for the demands of classroom management and instruction.

Although undergraduate course credits do not guarantee the quality of a prospective teacher, exposure to the major subject to be taught is critically important for secondary teachers. For example, do instructors in mathematics or English possess undergraduate majors or graduate credits in these fields, or did they complete more general undergraduate preparation?

Competence in Classroom Settings. The challenge of organizing and managing a classroom of 20-35 children or adolescents cannot be overemphasized. Because of the subtle nature of good teaching in this environment, indicators of competence in the classroom have, until recently, appeared beyond reach. But this is an important concern in the quality of teaching, and the emergence of the National Board for Professional Teaching Standards (and its efforts to develop reliable assessment procedures) promises to bring this critical area within sight.

Conditions of Teachers' Work

For too long, policymakers at all levels have considered teachers as interchangeable parts who could be shifted from one instructional setting to another. Recent research on effective schools, however, draws attention to very basic needs of teachers if they are to sustain their best efforts. Today's reform effort understands that better schools depend on teachers vested with greater authority to control classroom resources and determine curriculum and other core matters of their professional lives, backed by a supportive environment (see box on following page).

A PROFESSIONAL ENVIRONMENT FOR TEACHING

One of the most attractive aspects of professional work is the way professionals are treated in the workplace. Professionals are presumed to know what they are doing, and are paid to exercise their judgment.

"**Professional autonomy.** Professional autonomy is the first requirement. If the schools are to compete successfully with medicine, architecture, and accounting for staff, then teachers will have to have comparable authority in making the key decisions about the services they render. Within the context of a limited set of clear goals for students set by state and local policymakers, teachers, working together, must be free to exercise their professional judgment as to the best way to achieve these goals. This means the ability to make—or at least strongly influence—decisions concerning such things as the materials and instructional methods to be used, the staffing structure to be employed, the organization of the school day, the assignment of students, the consultants to be used, and the allocation of resources available to the school."

Source: A *Nation Prepared: Teachers for the 21st Century*. Carnegie Forum on Education and the Economy, May 1986.

The sub-concept of teachers' work includes the following important considerations.

Basic Classroom Resources. At the most basic level we find questions of minimal classroom resources for teaching, writing materials, and textbooks. Surprisingly, these are not uniformly available, particularly in many low-income urban and rural schools. But we also need to know if even modest discretionary funds to supplement basic classroom materials are available to teachers, and how many teachers spend their own income on public needs in order to provide classroom materials for their students.

Supporting Resources. Basic classroom resources are only the first step in building a professional working environment. Teachers must also have access to the supporting resources taken for granted by other professionals, mid-level managers, and even support staff: a private place to work outside the classroom; the flexibility to arrive at school early and to stay late; and access to library resources, telephones, photocopy machines, word processors, and the other "basics" of the telecommunications age.

Influence over Core Matters of Work. Maintaining efficacy in any professional's work implies controlling the core factors shaping that work. For teachers this means, at a minimum, selecting appropriate texts and materials, influencing acceptable norms for student and adult behavior within the school, and regular opportunities to meet with colleagues to discuss school matters.

Good Schools: Learning is a shared enterprise.

Support for Developing Teachers' Craft. A major theme of school restructuring is that schools must be learning places for teachers as well as students. Pre-service preparation is not an inoculation that is "good for life." Meaningful improvement in students' learning will not occur without a sustained commitment to staff development at each school site. This implies programs to assist new teachers and continuing staff development for experienced teachers. In colleges and universities this also implies consensus about the relative importance of time for undergraduate instruction, research, and public service.

Places of Purpose and Character

Good schools are not corporate franchises—identically stamped out across the countryside. Each is individually shaped, even owned, by those who spend their time in it—students, teachers, parents, and administrative staff.

Research tells us that good schools have a distinctive ethos, an organizational sense of mission that binds students, teachers, and staff to the school itself as a center for learning. Good schools are not confused about their purposes; their clarity of mission and sense of purpose are acute. These environments daily sustain teachers in their work, engage students in learning, and operate on the clear assumption that "in this building, everyone matters."

Schools with these features engage everyone in learning as a shared enterprise. For students, this means fewer incidents of class-cutting, absenteeism, and misbehavior. It means more time on homework and greater involvement in extracurricular activities. For teachers, it means spending extra time with students outside of class, attending school events at which they have no official obligations, and volunteering for committees and schoolwide assignments. It also means personal effort to improve their teaching through extra coursework and professional reading.

Clarity of Mission. People commit their best efforts if they feel they are part of something of value. If schools are to be communities of teaching and learning, at root must exist a sense of mission. This implies agreement about norms of instruction in terms of what should be taught, how it should be taught, and the academic and behavioral assumptions that govern students and teachers (see box).

SCHOOLS WITH CHARACTER

A 1990 report for the RAND Corporation examined parochial and public magnet secondary schools (focus schools) and comprehensive secondary schools (zoned schools) in New York City and compared their success in educating minority, low-income youngsters. The report attributed the success of the "focus" schools to the clarity of their mission and organizational structure. An excerpt from that document follows:

"The missions of focus and zoned public schools differ in the following ways:

- Focus schools concentrate on student outcomes to the virtual exclusion of all other matters. Zoned schools focus primarily on delivering programs and following procedures.

- Focus schools have a strong commitment to parenting, acting aggressively to mold student attitudes and values. Zoned schools see themselves primarily as transmitters of information and imparters of skills.

- Focus schools operate as problem-solving organizations, taking the initiative to change their programs in response to emerging needs. External mandates and rigid internal divisions of labor constrain the problem-solving capabilities of zoned schools.

- Focus schools sustain their own organizational character, both by attracting staff members who accept the school's premises and by socializing new staff members. Zoned schools have little capacity to select staff or influence the attitudes or behavior of new staff members.

In short, focus schools are designed to influence and change students. Zoned schools are designed to administer programs and deliver services."

Source: Paul T. Hill, et al., *High Schools with Character.* Santa Monica: RAND Corporation, 1990.

A Human Environment. Personal accounts of school dropouts describe schools as places that are often large, bureaucratic, and impersonal. In contrast, good schools are described as having a human scale in which concern for the students and cooperation are highly valued. Even if large, the ethic that "every student matters" is made real in the day-to-day life and interactions within the school. Teachers try to know and engage each student. Students believe that teachers are interested in them and care about their progress. Cooperation characterizes the relationships among adults as well.

Individual schools rarely control their own budgets or expenditures.

Basic Order and Safety. As the national goal of safe, disciplined, and drug-free schools acknowledges, teaching and learning cannot occur in an environment that lacks a stable social order and sense of safety. Reports from both schools and campuses indicate that this prerequisite is not always present. Schools and universities are very unusual social institutions. Like the home, the family, and the neighborhood, they encourage a sense of community, even intimacy. They cannot encourage that sense in a chaotic environment in which concern for personal well-being is ever-present.

Press Toward Academic Work. Good schools offer all students opportunities to engage rigorous academic material. But simply creating such opportunities is not enough. Good schools also structure their environment to press students to engage their material. One key factor here is teachers' expectations that all students can learn, and should learn.

School Resources

The panel has already commented on teachers' needs for classroom resources. The concept of "school resources" refers to the adequacy of the resources available to the school itself.

Individual schools rarely control their own budgets or expenditures. Teachers, professional staff, administrators, secretaries, and janitors are normally paid by the central school district which also allocates funds for most new construction, building equipment, maintenance, and supplies. This situation has encouraged one element of the reform movement to advocate "site-based" management, a concept under which school staff would, among other changes, control and allocate their own budgets.

The panel's interest in school resources has to do with developing indicators to ascertain whether most schools are well enough equipped to carry out their responsibilities. We suspect that many are not. Surveys within individual school districts have uncovered schools that might be closed as health or safety hazards if they were local production plants or restaurants. Unsanitary plumbing; broken toilets, banisters, and metal locker doors; and lead-based paint and other environmental hazards are present in many schools.

We believe that indicator data need to be developed around four sub-concepts:

- **Buildings:** What proportion of school buildings are unhealthy or unsafe because of environmental or other problems in the physical plant? Would most people in today's modern office be comfortable spending their working day in the typical school?

- **Libraries:** How adequate is the school's collection? Does it have a professional librarian? What are its hours during the school day? Does it have a regular, even if modest, acquisitions program? How much support does the library provide to teachers in their curriculum planning and to students trying to develop basic research skills?

- **Laboratories and Technology:** How up-to-date is the typical school in terms of its science laboratories, science equipment, and the technologies it can make available (e.g., personal computers) to support the instructional program?

- **Professional Personnel:** Professionals of various kinds—counselors, librarians, nurses—support instruction in most schools. What do professional groups believe is an adequate professional/student staffing ratio and how do most schools measure up to those standards?

Quality and Postsecondary Institutions

Many of the issues relevant to the quality of schools are equally appropriate to improvement of higher education institutions. Because the issues are framed in quite a different way in higher education, however, we have chosen to present them in a separate section.

Colleges and universities should, like schools, be places of purpose and character. This means providing humane environments with a press toward academic work. It means being student-centered. It also means that they should have a clear sense of mission and leadership that creates a vision shared by all members of the campus community. We need some gauge of the press to intellectual work on campus and its strength in relation to other forces on campus including fraternities, sororities, and the athletic culture.

There are several salient issues with regard to learning opportunities at the postsecondary level. At the most general level, we need to know how students sort themselves among different types of institutions—community colleges, proprietary institutions, and research universities—and the characteristics of students who gain access to institutions stressing undergraduate instruction. At a more detailed level, we need to know more about students' exposure to subject matter: How many are exposed to selected concepts (and in what depth) in key areas of core content?

Similarly, we need to know more about the integration of curricula. Because degrees are constructed from "courses" and "student credit hours" (often earned in more than one institution) there is a need to know how well integrated the course of studies is. At one level, it is important to understand how the offerings of 4-year campuses relate to transfer curricula in community colleges: What proportion of community college credits are lost in the transfer process? More fundamental is the question of the proportion of undergraduates who receive the benefit of a well-integrated general education curriculum.

At the college level, there is considerable concern about the amount of faculty time devoted to teaching, as opposed to research and public service, and about the nature and quality of undergraduate instruction. Many years of research tell us that good undergraduate education is characterized by high and clearly communicated expectations, by capstone experiences that require students to integrate and synthesize what they have learned, by opportunities to exercise and demonstrate skills, by frequent assessment and feedback to the student, by collaborative learning, and by frequent student-faculty contact outside the classroom setting. While there is need for more information about how faculty actually spend their time, there is an even greater need for information about the incidence of good educational practices and about the prevalence of conditions that encourage these practices (small class sizes/human scale, instruction by full-time rather than part-time faculty, and tenure policies that encourage teaching rather than research).

Finally, quality undergraduate instruction and research is difficult to deliver in the absence of adequate resources—libraries, computers and other equipment, physical plant, and research facilities and instrumentation. As with the schools, the nation needs indicators of the adequacy of resources available to support the academic tasks of colleges and universities.

Implications for Indicators

Some of the information the panel seeks in this issue area is already available. For example:

- NCES's Common Core of Data (CCD) includes state-by-state figures on numbers of teachers and pupil-teacher ratios, as well as on instructional aides, counselors, librarians, school and district administrators, and support staff.
- The Schools and Staffing Survey (SASS) and the National Educational Longitudinal Study (NELS:88) provide information on teacher preparation (e.g., degrees, certification status, experience, and course credits). SASS also includes teachers' self-reports on whether or not they are qualified in their fields of teaching assignment.
- CCSSO annually reports data on state requirements for teacher preparation and testing for teacher certification.
- Rough estimates of course-taking patterns, graduation requirements, exposure to subject matter, and time allocated to different subjects can be obtained from several sources including NAEP's High School Transcript Study, NELS:88, SASS, and IEA studies.
- The Integrated Postsecondary Education Data System (IPEDS), the core postsecondary education data collection program of NCES, collects data in areas such as institutional characteristics; enrollment; degree completion; salaries, tenure, and fringe benefits; revenues and expenditures; physical plant; and library collections.
- The College Student Experiences Questionnaire (CSEQ) provides useful student-reported data on student experience with various aspects of college life and self-assessments of knowledge and skills.[9]

But in other areas, our data sources are woefully inadequate. We have very little reliable information on instructional processes within the classroom. The extent of grouping and tracking practices within schools and classrooms, the use of peer-tutoring or cross-age tutoring, opportunities for collegial working relationships within the school, the quality of school leadership, and teachers' use of effective classroom management techniques are a mystery.

The quality of schools and colleges as educational institutions poses major challenges for indicator development and reporting. Good indicators in this domain must be grounded in the subtleties that define good instruction. Meaningful information will require deep

---

[9] CSEQ was developed at the Center for the Study of Evaluation, University of California, Los Angeles, under the direction of C. Robert Pace.

probes by subject matter, by grade, and by student background. We will need classroom observations on what students are actually asked to do, and samples of student work, including required tests and examinations. This topic is equally important at the postsecondary level. It should be possible to gain some insight into learning opportunities by classroom observation, by asking undergraduates about their experiences, and by examining the frequency of large lectures, smaller classes and laboratories, and the availability of seminars and tutorials for undergraduates.

Chapter 6

LEADING INDICATORS: TRENDS IN EDUCATION

As the panel argued in Chapter 3, policymakers at the national level rarely think about developing indicators of leading changes that affect the educational enterprise. The panel believes an indicator system can help monitor important changes and suggests two issue areas with considerable promise, readiness for school and societal support for learning.

It is no secret that the world of childhood is changing.

READINESS FOR SCHOOL

It is no secret that the world of childhood is changing. Many more children are growing up in single-parent families. At least one in four preschoolers (and one in five children under age 18) lives in poverty (see box on following page). The sharp increase in the number of working mothers and dual-career families means that child care and preschool play an increasingly critical role in children's early development.

The issues facing young children are especially critical and in many ways unique. If small children do not gain a sense of security, a capacity for human connections, and the foundations of cognitive skill in their first few years, the road before them is made that much more difficult.

The panel suggests two main concepts in the readiness area (see Figure 6 on page 85).

- the status of young children and their families—including the capabilities of children who are entering first grade, capabilities of 3-year-olds, and the health and family conditions of young children; and
- educational services in the early elementary grades as well as in kindergarten, preschool, and child care programs.

Status of Young Children and Their Families

The panel begins with information about what young children actually can do—their cognitive, socio-emotional, and physical capabilities. Despite the sensitivity of this issue, the panel believes it is essential to address the fundamental question of how ready children are for the demands of school.

A Profile of 3-Year-Olds and First Graders. The panel proposes a profile of the developmental progress of a representative sample of children who are entering first grade (i.e., 5- and 6-year-olds) and a sample of 3-year-olds. To gather some of the information the panel considers desirable, it will be necessary to assess the capabilities of samples of children, individually and in small groups, in sessions where the children respond to a series of tasks and games while skilled adults observe them.

We include 3-year-olds in these profiles for two reasons. First, profound changes in the economic conditions of young children

---

THE GROWTH OF POVERTY

Although the poverty rate among children under the age of 18 declined from 26% to 14.9% between 1960 and 1970, it has been inching steadily upward since that time. Minority children are two to three times as likely as white children to be raised in low-income households.

Children Under 18 Living in Poverty

Source: In 1990 *Condition of Education* (U.S. Department of Education). Data from *Poverty in the United States*, Washington: Bureau of the Census, 1989.

necessitate a sharper understanding of today's 3-year-olds if schools are to appropriately serve tomorrow's first graders. Second, a developmental perspective on children's growth requires information from different points in time. Changes in capabilities between age 3 and the first grade will tell us a great deal about the effectiveness of current services for children.

Other Factors in Readiness. Additional data on important factors that powerfully influence readiness—e.g., health, nutrition, weight at birth—must also be collected. Information about the health conditions of newborns provides the first warning of potential educational problems and a benchmark of the nation's progress in addressing prenatal risk factors. We propose gathering information on the incidence of low birthweight babies, out-of-wedlock births, and births to chemically dependent mothers, teenagers, and to mothers who received little or no prenatal care.

Figure 6

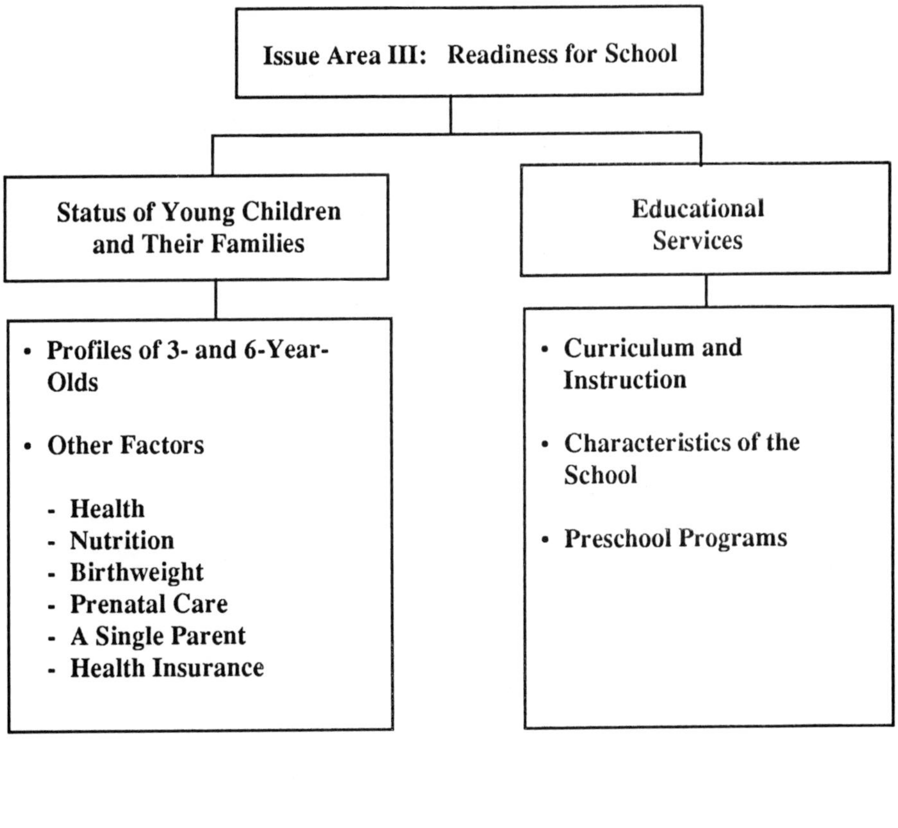

The school itself may need to be "fixed" to work with children.

Because health care in early childhood can forestall many educational problems, we also propose reporting on immunization rates and coverage by health insurance. Similarly, we propose reporting on the availability of nutrition and health services for pregnant women, infants, and young children. These data should be collected in such a way that policymakers can obtain relevant information on such factors as numbers of young children living in poverty, percent of families receiving Aid to Families with Dependent Children, level of maternal education, family structure, mother's age at birth of first child, incidence of drug or alcohol abuse, and level of participation in parent education programs.

Educational Services

Schools must also be ready to accommodate the strengths and weaknesses of incoming students. If we neglect the issue of schools' readiness on the assumption that children should fit the school, our society runs the risk of emphasizing children's deficits. When there is a mismatch between young children's capabilities and the school's demands, the school itself needs to be "fixed" to work with these children in a developmentally appropriate way.

Curriculum and Instruction. We propose sub-concepts of early elementary curriculum and instructional strategies. These include the extent to which schools provide the following opportunities: the chance to learn skills in a context that is meaningful, to learn through play, to learn through concrete hands-on activities, to receive instruction tailored to unique needs, to learn in small groups, to experience both active and quiet learning activities, and to learn through multi-sensory instruction. The panel also proposes indicators of the amount of time spent by young children in classes with the low student/teacher ratios that are warranted according to educational research. Further, we propose indicators of elementary teachers' training in early childhood education as well as of the safety and comfort of young children's learning environments.

Characteristics of the School. A meaningful "school readiness" indicator system will measure not simply classroom environments but also characteristics of the school itself: the extent to which schools screen students from school or retain them in early grades; the extent and nature of parent involvement during children's early elementary school years; elementary schools' collaboration with preschools; and school cooperation with community agencies that provide health care, social services, and other forms of assistance.

Preschool Programs. Finally, we propose indicators of the services provided before first grade—including kindergarten, preschools, and child care—and the numbers of students receiving these services. The Perry Preschool Study has captured widespread attention with its findings on the many benefits of an intensive preschool program, including persistence in school and reduced delinquency.[10] However it must be remembered that few preschool programs are comparable in intensity and, arguably, quality to that program.

An indicator system that examines the services offered by a sample of preschools can help us to understand the overall quality of educational services available to particular populations of young children as well as the key differences among programs provided to different children. Thus, we recommend measuring and reporting aspects of the preschool curriculum, such as the degree of academic emphasis and the intensity and nature of parent involvement. We also recommend collecting data about program staffing—including adult/child ratios, staff training, and staff turnover.

Further, we recommend some simpler indicators related to preschool education. These include enrollment levels, ages and duration of participation, numbers of children who receive no preschool education, and participation in full- and half-day kindergarten.

[10] Schweinhart, L.J., & Weikart, D.P., "Young children grow up: The effects of the Perry Preschool Program on youths through age 15." Ypsilanti, Michigan: High/Scope Press, 1980.

Implications for Indicators

A wide variety of public and private groups are already collecting some of the information the panel considers important in the school readiness area. For example:

- The Center for the Study of Social Policy has published national and state-level data on indicators of "child and family well-being," including three different measures of infant health—percent of births to mothers without prenatal care in the first trimester; percent of low-birthweight babies; and the number of deaths under one year of age per 1,000 births.

- The National Center for Health Statistics provides information on medical care and incidence of health insurance, and the Bureau of Census provides information on the number of households without health insurance, broken down by household composition and age of children.

- The Bureau of the Census' Current Population Survey (CPS) collects data each year on enrollment of 3-, 4-, and 5-year-olds in pre-primary educational programs with further breakdowns by family income and ethnicity.

- The Southern Regional Education Board's "Challenge 2000" report provides data, by state, on state-funded educational programs for pre-kindergarten children.

But the fact remains that data on preschool and kindergarten programs, as well as information on program-home instructional interaction, are not nearly as extensive for young children as they are for children enrolled in elementary and secondary schools. Improving the information data base for very young children will be a formidable task, but one that promises significant benefits.

One particular aspect of the panel's suggestions with respect to school readiness deserves elaboration. The panel recommends a profile of 3-year-olds and of first-grade students (5 or 6 years old). In proposing these profiles, we wish to make it clear that although some assessments of sample groups of children will be involved, the panel is not suggesting traditional tests. As noted above, it will be necessary to assess the capabilities of children, individually and in small groups, in sessions where the children respond to a series of tasks and games, and skilled adults observe what the children do. Members of the panel recognize the controversial nature of these testing proposals and the history of many efforts to screen children out of first grade or kindergarten on the basis of "readiness tests." The panel does not endorse or propose such tests, and we reject the terms "screening" or "readiness tests" as a characterization of the assessments we propose.

The proposed assessments could not be used to screen individual children because no one would have access to data about individual performance on the assessment. The samples should be designed to give an accurate picture of the capabilities of the entire school-entering population, the entire population of 3-year-olds, and important subgroups such as new first graders from impoverished families. These subgroups would be selected, for example, to identify for policymakers the kinds of children—but not individual children—who may need special services.

In addition, the assessments would be broad-based measures of student readiness rather than "tests" according to the usual connotation of the term. Instead, these assessments would measure numerous dimensions of readiness—including neurological development, sensorimotor skills, attitudes, and social capabilities—as well as cognitive skills. And, they would allow children to communicate in various ways, including speaking, pointing, manipulating objects, and, if they are able to do so, writing.

SOCIETAL SUPPORT FOR LEARNING

This issue area combines a number of traditional concerns about financial support of schools and colleges with issues that are relatively new to discussions of indicators, such as the amount of time parents give to schools and children's learning activities. At the broadest level, this issue area addresses contributions made by society and subgroups of society—the family, the individual, and organizations outside schools—to education. While these non-financial topics raise some new directions for indicator development, they have already attracted the attention of national leaders. For example, materials accompanying the development of the national goals and AMERICA 2000 speak of:

- parents' obligations to be "interested and involved in their children's education;"
- the vital role expected of "communities, business, and civic groups;" and

- "communities where learning can happen" in which the "other 91%" of student time outside school supports learning.

"Societal support for learning" incorporates four components: (1) the role of the family as educator, (2) community support for learning, (3) the educational effects of American culture, and (4) the nature of financial assistance to *all* educating institutions from *all* types of sources (see Figure 7).

Figure 7

Issue Area IV: Societal Support for Learning			
Family Support for Learning	**Community Support for Learning**	**Cultural Support for Learning**	**Financial Support for Learning**
• Parental Attitudes and Involvement at Home • Parental Responsibility for Basic Care • Parental Involvement with the School	• Libraries • Subject-Specific Community Support - Science - Mathematics - Arts - Humanities - Languages - Social Sciences	• Citizen Attitudes and Voting Behavior • Adult Behavior: Reading Patterns • Societal Competition with Learning	• Revenues • Expenditures • Other Educating Institutions' Revenues and Expenditures

Family Support for Learning

Traditional measures of home environments conducive to learning have often focused on possessions—books, desks, computers, and the like. We advocate paying greater attention to specific values and specific types of parent-child and parent-school interactions. Four areas seem especially important:

Parental Attitudes and Involvement at Home. How much do parents value learning in itself and how important do they believe education is for their children's futures? How much control do they

90

believe their children have over their own educational achievement (e.g., the role of "hard work" vs. "innate" capacity)? How do they define a "good education" (e.g., the acquisition of a diploma or of specific dispositions and skills)? What are their expectations for how much education their children will complete? Such basic attitudes, broken down by background characteristics, are fundamental indices of parental priorities and willingness to exert energy on behalf of learning.

How important do parents believe education is for their children's future?

Similar issues arise when we turn to parent-as-teacher within the home. What kind of instructional assistance do parents provide their children, including checking on homework, tutoring, discussing ideas, visiting cultural institutions, and encouraging leisure reading? An increasing number of items on surveys contain data from parents about such matters, which eventually might be combined into some composite indicator of parental involvement in instruction.

Parental Responsibility for Basic Care. The theme here is nurturance from birth through adolescence as a basic obligation of parenthood. Are the numbers of parents who provide the nurturing basics—getting children to school, providing food, clothing, shelter, health care and adult supervision—increasing or decreasing? Data on school attendance and the amount of time children are at home without adult supervision are two examples of measures that bear on this theme.

Parental Involvement with the School. The home side of the home-school connection looks for indicators of how well parents take advantage of opportunities to involve themselves in school-sponsored activities and school affairs in general. Measures should focus on actual participation rates of parents, not on theoretical "opportunities" to participate. Examples include parental participation in volunteer school-day programs, in outside events such as fund-raising and parents' associations, and in governance committees of various kinds.

The school side of this equation is equally important. The nature of social and family change in the United States means that today there are fewer opportunities for informal contact between parents and teachers. School professionals increasingly are accepting responsibility for engaging parents in their children's education. Their mission includes working with parents to foster more productive home-school collaboration.

Community Support for Learning

The construct of "community support" embraces most of the educational institutions and programs outside the formal education system. Virtually everyone experiences, and is deeply influenced by, some sort of family or primary care unit, but many important educative agencies cannot be accommodated in most indicator systems because there are too many of them, each experienced by only a few individuals. Comprehensive coverage is impossible. But an educational indicator system must concern itself with all educative agencies that help students develop their talent.

Two types of institutions or programs seem especially pertinent: libraries and other programs that enrich specific subjects such as science or the arts and humanities.

Libraries. Our principal concerns are the availability of library resources, how libraries are being used, how much they are being used, and by whom. A vital indicator system needs information about all four topics. Libraries can be used as places to read, study, look, and listen; they are also sources of materials that can be borrowed and used elsewhere. They organize a variety of diverse programs on every conceivable subject. The challenge is not simply to get aggregate figures on library usage but to speak more precisely to who uses libraries for which purposes. We want to know, for example, whether their use as sanctuaries for study by inner-city school children is increasing or decreasing. We want to know which materials circulate most—what the market is—and how this differs by location and constituency.

School libraries are also important. Their quality should be assessed in Issue Area 2 (Quality of Educational Institutions) and the information collected there (e.g., the use of school libraries for support of assignments and homework) can be cross-referenced with services available in community libraries.

Subject-Specific Community Support for Learning. The organizing principle here is not the educating agency—e.g., museums—but content areas. In science, mathematics, the arts, humanities, social sciences, and languages, the central questions are: What agencies or programs exist outside schools and colleges to develop interest, skill, and knowledge? How much participation is there in these programs? Who participates? How, if at all, are the programs linked to schools so that some continuity and reinforcement occurs?

The same set of questions apply to all of these subject-centered areas. Where is the societal support for learning in each one? How much participation is there? Who participates? How are programs linked to schools and colleges? Art museums, math clubs, music organizations, corporate outreach efforts in science, and political and youth service groups deserve attention. A key general questions is: How much of society's concern for *learning* has been subtly deemphasized in schools and given over to more specialized external agencies?

Faith in education does not imply a deep respect for learning.

Cultural Support for Learning

For more than a century foreign observers have marvelled at America's limitless faith in education and its willingness to expend vast sums to make educational opportunities for all youth a major social objective. But at the same time, many observers have noted that our faith in education does not necessarily imply a deep respect for learning. More education, not necessarily more learning, is valued as a principal means for Americans to advance economically.

It is imperative that an education indicator system take account of the educational values of the American culture, since these values have practical consequences for both tangible support and the attitudes of American youth toward learning. What, in short, is the cultural ethos concerning education within which all educational institutions operate and which, in part, shapes the educational attitudes and behavior of youth?

Citizen Attitudes and Voting Behavior. Over time polls of public attitudes about education provide informative benchmarks of public satisfaction or concern with school and college performance. Parallels can be found in economics where consumer expectations and degree of economic confidence are regularly surveyed. We recommend identification of a consistent set of items for polls that would track changing public attitudes about the condition of education, preschool through postsecondary, and about key enduring concerns expressed throughout this report.

Voting behavior on education issues (e.g., school bonds and tax limitation initiatives) is another important tool to track the electorate's educational interests. To be useful, analyses must relate particular issues to voter background characteristics.

Adult Behavior: Reading Patterns. Reading as an independent pursuit is a key indicator of an educated society. What are the reading habits of adults and youth, and how have they changed? Surveys of reading offer many insights into how well adults emulate the behavior they expect the education system to instill in youth. We have apparently been more successful instilling the ability to read than instilling the wish to read material that goes beyond how-to and pop-culture books and magazines. Newspaper readership has fallen considerably. International comparisons in this area would reveal how American society may differ from other industrialized nations in what reading habits we value. Regional or community comparisons might also expose wide differences in reading patterns within the United States.

Societal Competition with Learning. Many providers of goods and services vie with educational institutions for the interest, time, and dollars of youth. It is completely appropriate for an indicator system to examine how well its competition is doing—how much is invested in those elements of youth culture that might instill habits of consumption and behavior potentially at odds with the central tasks of schools and colleges.

The panel advocates data collection that would better establish the linkages between high frequencies of TV watching and employment and actual school and college performance. Further, we believe greater attention needs to be paid to the behavior of the youth culture industry, not just the behavior of youth. How do expenditures directed at influencing the buying behaviors of young people compare with school expenditures? How does adolescent consumer spending compare with education expenditures on youth?

Financial Support for Learning

In this area abundant data of many types exist. But in spite of long-standing questions about educational finance—e.g., whether society provides sufficient and equitable support for schools and colleges—information about the nation's fiscal investment in education remains less than satisfying. The relationship between fiscal measures and measures of school performance remains inconclusive. We call for measures of financial effort and expenditure that emphasize readily understandable links with the instructional arena and with the allocation of resources to educational agencies and to students.

The traditional approach of measuring dollar inputs and their general distribution needs to be supplemented with an emphasis on what dollars actually buy and how these expenditures are related to program quality, organization, and student learning. How, for example, are resources used within curricular areas and among students within the school or campus, and how are they distributed between teaching and administration?

Revenues. How are sources of support shifting among local, state, and federal governments, as well as between rigidly prescribed and more flexible funding mandates? Recent decades have seen noticeable shifts in patterns of support for public schools; in particular, the proportion of school support from local resources has gone down while state support has gone up. During the 1980s, also, corporate support to schools (in the form of collaborative programs) increased substantially. How much has the corporate sector invested in these initiatives? Private schools, barred from most direct and indirect public assistance and generally ignored by corporate America, relied more heavily on gifts, above and beyond tuition, from their own constituencies.

Higher education (both public and private) is supported by a somewhat broader and more complicated revenue mix than elementary/secondary education, but the same reorientation regarding how the dollars are used is required. Different levels of government provide direct or indirect support (e.g., student aid and indirect research expense recovery), while a complex mix of voluntary giving supplements direct tuition payments. We need to know about changing patterns in the share of expenses borne by students and families on the one hand, and government, institutions, and the voluntary sector on the other.

Equally important, we need information that will provide greater insight into which methods of distributing these resources—directly to institutions or indirectly through student assistance—are most effective in accomplishing public policy objectives. Finally, there is a need to establish indicators that reflect the basic economic factors, including price and productivity, that are central to policymaking about education.

Expenditures. Most revenues in the private school sector are unrestricted, but a significant fraction of public school funding at all levels must be spent on specific programs. Per-pupil-expenditure figures must be demystified; they are misleading because they often bear little relation to actual dollars expended on particular types of students in particular programs.

One useful step is to separate school-site expenditures into those that support the teaching staff and those that support administration. NCES is already moving in this direction and should plan additional breakdowns at least by elementary and secondary levels. Even more targeted breakdowns (e.g., expenditures for math and science, athletics, and extracurricular activities) would provide a much better understanding of where dollars go. These breakdowns can inform the debate about whether excessive dollars go to central bureaucracies or extracurricular activities.

Postsecondary education should continue to disaggregate per student expenditures so that dollars spent for instruction are clearly shown. The mixed purposes of much of postsecondary education—in which research and service play roles as significant as instruction—

require clear monitoring of where dollars are actually spent at a time when the instructional quality of higher education has been under increasing scrutiny.

We endorse careful comparisons of teacher salaries with salaries (beginning, average, and high) for other occupations requiring bachelors degrees, and then comparing these relationships with those of other major industrialized countries. The same comparisons might be made for school principals. Such data, for both public and private schools, bear directly on the nation's commitment to education, as well as on more immediate issues of teacher attrition. Finally, the case for scrutiny of faculty and administrator salaries—in comparison with similar occupations—applies equally in the area of postsecondary education.

In the context of postsecondary expenditures, data on the availability of student financial aid (including graduate study) should be collected, as well as family and student indebtedness stemming from education expenditures. Financial aid availability in private schools, institutional effort to provide financial aid in such schools, and indebtedness resulting from private elementary and secondary education should be incorporated into this analysis.

Other Educating Institutions. No consideration of financial support for learning could be complete without examining the investment made in educative agencies that are not part of the official public and private "system" of schools and colleges. These include libraries, museums, youth and church groups with educational programs, adult learning centers, and the like. Collectively, this is an enormous productive force in American education. Its funding is sometimes public, sometimes private, sometimes mixed. We need better revenue and expenditure information on these institutions as well.

On the revenue side, we need a much better idea of the sheer scale of this sector: What aggregated financial resources are devoted to it and from which sources do they come? This question goes beyond a simplistic public-private breakdown—it needs disaggregation of public monies at the local, state and federal level And it clearly needs disaggregation when the monies are voluntary contributions from individuals, corporations, and foundations.

On the expenditure side, the main issue is to learn which dollars support which types of learning endeavors. For example, how much money—and for what kinds of programs, and from which sources—supports the development of science interests and art skills among young children, adolescents, and young adults? How do these expenditures compare to what schools and colleges do for the same age groups in the same fields? This line of questioning should produce indicators that give a better, more balanced sense of the total societal contribution to learning, subject by subject.

Americans have defined education as what happens in schools and colleges.

Implications for Indicators

With the exception of revenue and expenditure information in traditional educating institutions, most concepts outlined above have rarely been regarded as education indicators. Americans have tended to ignore learning outside the formal enterprise and to define education as what happens in schools and colleges. One significant implication of the panel's formulation, therefore, is the attempt to establish linkages between and among the health of families, community educative institutions, broader cultural attitudes, and the health of education. All are, in fact, part of a single "system." The nation's choice is to make this system coherent or maintain its current fragmentation.

Another implication for indicator development is that much of the most essential information is neither regularly collected nor easily expressed by such summary measures as dollars, percentages, or scores. For example, the key indicator issue within the family support construct is not changing family demographics (e.g., increases in single-parent or dual-career families) but how families—whatever their makeup—nurture learning and participate in the learning process. A reliable indicator in this area would emphasize not family composition but specific family values and parent-child and parent-school interactions.

A third implication for indicator development is the importance of examining and quantifying *relationships* among school and non-school educational influences. It is the positive interaction among and across various educative institutions (called "configurations" of learning by the late historian Lawrence A. Cremin) that indicates health—not simply the discrete existence of one education program or specific educational opportunity. School-based surveys of students and families can be an efficient means of learning about out-of-school *educational* activities of students and how these activities connect the community and the school. Such surveys should attend more closely to matters of this sort, and not remain preoccupied with television viewing and paid employment as the only indicators of how youth spend their time outside school.

Finally, we recognize that useful indicators of the culture's support (or lack of support) of education will inevitably be provocative. Many institutions in American society would prefer to remain aloof from any indicator system that suggests they can be part of the solution and may, perhaps, be part of the problem. The panel believes that it is wholly appropriate to assess the *competition* with education, and that this is a wide-open field which has never before been properly mapped.

There are, for example, large and powerful forces in America simultaneously opposed to control of handguns and in favor of safe schools. It is, of course, conceivable that schools could be safe with firearms all around them. But it is hardly likely and this situation undermines the schools' efforts to teach. In similar fashion, major elements of the youth and adult cultures ridicule young people who take education seriously (e.g., "math nerds") while lionizing athletic accomplishment. Issues such as these, in the panel's view, are fair game for a genuine education indicator system. If the panel's framework is implemented, it will step on some powerful toes. Motion pictures, television, the music business, the entire teen consumer product industry will be examined through an educational not an economic lens. But that is the challenge of this framework: Education has foes as well as friends, and an indicator information system needs to pay attention to both.

Education has foes as well as friends and an indicator system needs to pay attention to both.

99

Chapter 7

VALUES AND ASPIRATIONS

The panel has argued consistently that the most powerful system of indicators will start from the perspective of what consumers and the public expect and need from education (learner outcomes and high quality institutions), and then incorporate leading indicators related to education (readiness for school and societal support for learning). But the people of the United States also clearly expect the nation's schools and colleges to advance certain national values above and beyond the benefits education provides to individual students.

As noted in Chapter 3, the panel believes a comprehensive indicator information system should incorporate national values and aspirations and be broad enough to accommodate shifts in national priorities. Two issue areas appear to be most promising: education and economic productivity, and equity in American education.

EDUCATION AND ECONOMIC PRODUCTIVITY

The panel believes four central concepts form the foundation for a system of indicators on this topic: the education pipeline, economic consequences of education, workplace support for skill development, and research and development (see Figure 8 on following page).

The Formal Education Pipeline

The education system is frequently compared to a "pipeline," a metaphor for the supply of people with the skills and knowledge needed by the workplace. The pipeline metaphor, by emphasizing the progress of youth and adults through formal educational institutions and critical milestones, offers a picture of the developing supply of new labor for the workforce. The longitudinal studies that follow individuals over a period of years, and which NCES has sponsored

new labor for the workforce. The longitudinal studies that follow individuals over a period of years, and which NCES has sponsored

Figure 8

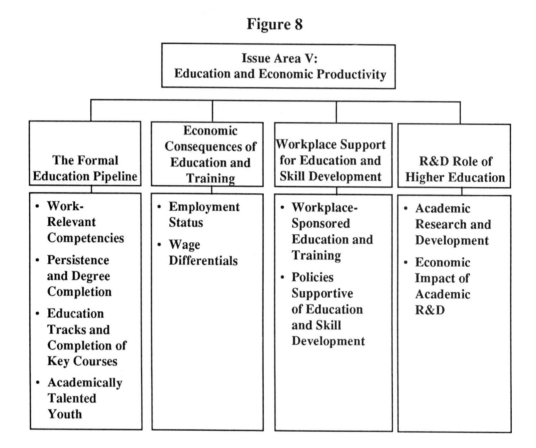

over the past decade, offer an ideal resource for illuminating how well the pipeline operates for different groups in our society.

Four aspects of the pipeline are most significant: (1) work-relevant competencies; (2) persistence and completion; (3) educational tracks and completion of key courses; and (4) the development of academically talented youth.

Work-Relevant Competencies. Which types of knowledge and skills are essential for today's workplace and that of the future? There is no simple response to this question, nor is there a definitive source of such information. In recent years several prestigious groups have put forth lists that confirm the importance of particular work-relevant competencies—reading, communication, mathematics, basic as well as complex reasoning, use of information, self-direction, effective teamwork, a commitment to craft, and adaptability to change. These competencies form an important part of what we defined earlier as Learner Outcomes. We repeat them here to emphasize that these competencies are important not only as essential ends of education but also as a means toward enhancing national productivity.

Persistence in School and Completion of Degrees. The number of students dropping out of school is an indicator of how many young people are not acquiring the competencies needed by the economy. We must routinely monitor counts of youth who drop out of school during the K-12 years as well as at the postsecondary level. Over the last decade slight declines in the percentage of youth who drop out of high school have been evident; but nationwide a sizable number (in 1989, more than four million youth between the ages of 16 and 24) are not in school and have not completed high school.

In the past we have emphasized the high school years in our concerns about youth staying in school, but we need to extend our focus to earlier ages as children make the transition from grade to middle schools or junior highs, and from there into high school. Equally important is the need to extend our sights to older age groups to track both the enrollment and persistence of persons in postsecondary institutions.

Information about persistence needs to be complemented by knowledge about students' completion of degrees and advanced degrees. Measures providing this information need to identify individuals who return to finish their diplomas and degrees at later points. At the postsecondary level, routine measures of average credit hours earned by degree earners, and the years it takes to earn a degree, are needed to assess changes in the dynamics of completing college and the changing requirements attached to that segment of the pipeline.

Educational Tracks and Completion of Key Courses. A national indicator system needs to keep the public informed about which paths of study secondary students are pursuing—vocational, college preparatory, or general—in order that the public can combine

Which types of knowledge and skills are essential for today's workplace and that of the future?

accumulated suggesting that these youth face the worst employment prospects once they leave school. We cannot rely on students as the sole reporters of educational paths; rather, we need objective measures that delve more deeply into the sequence and content of courses that students take.

Youth who fail to complete algebra by the end of 9th grade may face serious obstacles in college.

There is also a need for information that helps us address such questions at the level of specific courses. Youth who fail to complete specific academic courses at key points in their schooling—for example, algebra by the end of 9th grade—face serious obstacles to later success in college. With respect to proficiency in science and technology, we need to monitor the exposure of youth throughout the pipeline (including elementary school) to these subjects.

At the postsecondary level, information about enrollment and completion of degrees in critical areas such as science, engineering, computer science, and mathematics needs to reach the public routinely. Particularly relevant are measures that track graduate study and the award of advanced degrees to U.S. students and those from other countries. Recent trends indicate that enrollments of U.S citizens in graduate science and engineering programs have not increased since 1986, while foreign enrollments in these programs have increased. A critical piece of this picture is whether these graduates settle in their countries of origin or in the United States.

Academically Talented Youth. The national economy of the future is likely to depend not only on improved competence among all youth; it also needs those with the greatest academic promise to develop their talents to the fullest. A major pipeline issue is whether our system of formal schooling is able to retain these youth and extend their academic potential. Identifying such youth is not without controversy, but no one doubts they exist and that they span the categories of race, gender, ethnic origin, and income. A combination of assessment results, possibly amplified by teacher judgments, provides an approach to identifying such youth. The key areas to monitor are the courses pursued by such students (e.g., Advanced Placement), enrollment in postsecondary schools, persistence, major fields pursued, graduate or professional study, and degree completion.

Economic Consequences of Education and Training

The pipeline metaphor addresses the supply of skilled people. Equally important is the demand picture. There is no simple way of assessing workplace demand for specific types of skills and proficiencies because employers adjust to the supply by restructuring work and employing workers with different levels of skill. It is, therefore, difficult to measure how the supply of skilled workers matches the needs of the workplace, but we need to make a start. Two workplace responses, however, appear promising: (l) the employment status of persons with different levels of education, and (2) differences in the wages paid to individuals from different educational backgrounds.

Employment Status. The key question in this sub-concept is whether youth and young adults with different educational backgrounds find gainful employment. Unemployment statistics broken down by whether youth have dropped out or completed high school, or whether they have completed 2- or 4-year colleges or trade schools, offer an indication of the value of education in the economy. These traditional measures need to be expanded with routine mapping of unemployment among persons with different competencies and fields of preparation. Equally important is the need to move beyond current definitions of participation in the labor force to incorporate people who no longer seek employment. This is particularly relevant for high school dropouts, who are among the most likely to leave the labor force for long periods of time.

One valuable indicator to track is employment in a job or field for which a person has trained. Thus, for special vocational training (e.g., automotive mechanics) or advanced scientific degrees (e.g., physics), employment in jobs where the specialized training is utilized provides an important signal of demand—a demand which is likely to influence decisions of current students.

Wage Differentials. While trends in employment patterns roughly reflect workplace preferences for particular types of educated workers, wage differences are somewhat more informative because they add the element of price. In an economy with few people of working age to fill available jobs, unemployment levels across all types of educated workers may not show much difference. But if workplace demand for specific skills is increasing faster than the supply of people with such skills, wage differences among workers should begin to widen over time.

Wage differentials based on years of schooling and credentials have been tracked for some time (see box on following page). Recently they have been used in conjunction with information about the number of college graduates to demonstrate the economy's growing demand for college-educated workers. Measures of wage differences reflecting proficiency levels are especially useful as indicators of whether employers value youths' skills and competence or their credentials.

Workplace Support for Education and Skills

Employers can play a significant role in the development of an educated workforce by subsidizing short-term, job-related training and by adopting policies that support schools' and parents' efforts to educate children. This dual role frames the types of workplace support that should be reflected in a national system of indicators.

Businesses are unlikely to invest in general training if they risk losing trained employees to other companies.

Workplace Sponsored Education and Training. As the 21st century approaches, corporate America may need to expand training for both job entrants and adult workers. Many observers expect that, in the future, employees will need intermittent training to deal with new technologies. Shrinking numbers of skilled new job entrants will increase the pressure on employers to provide training to American workers and to immigrants. At the same time, there are strong pressures on employers to vest these responsibilities in other sectors of society. Experts suggest that businesses are unlikely to invest significantly in general training if they risk losing trained employees to other companies. It is also important to monitor trends in the types of training employers provide (e.g., basic skills, technical, or managerial) and who receives each type of training.

Workplace Policies Supportive of Education. A national system of indicators also needs to capture the links between business and schools that promote the alignment of formal education with requirements of the workplace. School-business partnerships are

ARE SCHOOLING AND LEARNING WORTH THE EFFORT?

Is education worth the time and perseverance required to obtain a high school or college diploma? It certainly is. Two separate analyses underline the economic value of staying in school and performing at high levels:

Returns to Education*
(Average wages of schooling group relative to average wages of next-lower schooling group)

Time Period	High School	Some College	College	Graduate School
All Experience Groups				
1963-68	10.7%	16.7%	31.4%	13.6%
1969-74	9.5	17.1	34.2	14.2
1975-80	11.0	12.0	33.8	16.9
1981-86	14.2	14.8	37.6	17.7
1-5 Years experience				
1963-68	18.8%	12.7%	26.7%	10.9%
1969-74	14.2	8.9	30.4	12.8
1975-80	17.2	8.3	22.6	12.6
1981-86	19.3	14.5	34.1	12.6

The Value of Achievement in High School**

Average annual earnings between 1978 and 1980 by high school graduation status and level of academic skills.

Academic Skills Level	Males' Earnings ($)		Females' Earnings($)	
	Dropouts	Graduates	Dropouts	Graduates
Lowest quintile	4,616	6,013	1,429	2,936
Second lowest quintile	6,595	8,039	2,156	4,235
Middle quintile	6,765	8,190	3,102	4,629
Second highest quintile	8,321	9,433	2,465	5,469
Highest quintile	9,086	10,738	4,145	6,003

*   Murphy, Kevin and Finis Welch, "Wage Premiums for College Graduates," Educational Researcher, May, 1989.

**   Berlin, Gordon and Andrew Sum, *Toward a More Perfect Union: Basic Skills, Poor Families, and Our Economic Future.* New York: Ford Foundation, 1988 recent manifestations of such links, but partnerships are an inadequate concept for framing the needed set of indicators. What indicators need to capture are the types of activities in which schools and businesses join to link their common needs: apprenticeships, mentoring programs, instructors from the business community, achievement recognition programs, curriculum task forces, and the like. Of major interest is the sustained nature of these joint endeavors and their overall magnitude, both in the community and nationwide. Monitoring trends in the proportion of companies that consider an applicant's academic record in school as a factor in hiring—or that have written policies permitting time off for parent/teacher conferences—can also indicate the extent to which the private sector endorses the value of learning.

Higher Education's Research and Development Role

Institutions of higher education serve as the primary source of highly skilled, expert members of the workforce. Less obvious is their contribution to the pool of ideas and know-how that supports innovation and increased productivity. Industries in the United States depend on universities to conduct basic research which they then draw on and adapt in their own laboratories and development units.

Academic R&D. Recent estimates indicate that academic research and development constitutes only around 11 percent of all U.S. research and development spending, but a much larger proportion of basic research expenditures. The exact proportion is hard to estimate because a great deal of academic research is funded by universities themselves—in their payment of salaries to regular faculty who do research as well as teaching. We need better data on how faculty spend their time, as well as how this allocation of time is related to research output. Much R&D, particularly externally funded R&D, occurs in science and engineering disciplines. Technology and economies of scale in these fields cause basic R&D efforts to be concentrated in a relatively small number of institutions where equipment, library collections, and brainpower can coalesce to extend knowledge and its applications.

Research in graduate programs contributes to the development of graduate-level scientists, doctors, and engineers, for without access to ideas at the cutting edge these individuals will be less prepared for assuming roles in tomorrow's society and training others to apply technological advances. The public needs to have information that enables it to compare trends in the amount of R&D occurring in higher education with trends in the quality of teaching.

Economic Impact of Academic R&D. We need, however, to go beyond simply tracking the amount and whereabouts of academic R&D. We also need indicators that reflect the impact of this R&D on our national economic well-being. Developing such measures will not be simple, but there are some clues as to where to begin. One notion is to track corporate support of academic research. This affords one limited perspective on how much corporations value academic research. Another piece of evidence can be obtained from surveys of firms to gather judgments from corporate leaders about the role of academic research in the development of new products and processes. The National Science Board in 1989 reported on one prototype survey indicating that leaders in the pharmaceuticals industry attribute almost half of new products to recent academic research.[11] Also useful in this connection may be an expansion of studies analyzing changes in R&D expenditures and related changes in productivity and growth over time, as well as those examining international differences in R&D activities, productivity, and growth. Additional research may produce other measures of the aggregate economic impact of higher education's R&D efforts which may help the public better gauge the interdependence that exists between research and the health of the economy.

Leaders in the pharmaceuticals industry attribute almost half of new products to recent academic research.

Implications for Indicators

This is an issue area in which considerable information is available for some sub-concepts but very little useful information is available for others. Among existing sources of information, for example, we can draw on:

- Analyses conducted by SCANS, the U.S. Department of Labor, the American Society on Training and Development,

[11] National Science Board, *Science and Engineering Indicators, 1989.* Washington, D.C.: National Science Board, 1989 (NSB89-1).

and the RAND Corporation on workplace skills or on employer-sponsored training.

- Periodic projections from the Bureau of Labor Statistics (BLS) on the employment outlook in broad occupational groups according to years of education (high attainment group, where two-thirds of employees possess one or more years of college; middle attainment group, with occupations requiring at least 12 years of school; and a low attainment group, where more than a third of employees have less than 12 years of school).

- Periodic reports from the National Science Foundation on advanced degrees earned—particularly in engineering, the physical and biological sciences, and the social sciences—as well as on academic R&D.

But it is clear that much more needs to be done in this issue area. In particular, the panel believes that assessment of work-relevant competencies should correspond with the critical transition points defining the formal education pipeline: the end of primary school, middle school, high school, and college, and entry into and progress in the early years of work. In this regard, we have competency measures in traditional subjects in grades 4, 8, and 12. However, much more attention needs to be given to assessing the competencies of young adults.

A Young Adult Assessment. Developing a national young adult assessment (ages 24-30) of skills, knowledge and dispositions is vitally important to focusing attention on the proficiencies of school dropouts, as well as high school and college graduates. Deciding which competencies are needed, both now and in the future, is likely to remain an inexact art as work-relevant competencies shift in response to technical, labor, and market influences. The Department of Labor's SCANS group recently has accepted a charge to identify the skills needed in the workplace, acceptable levels of proficiency, and effective means of measuring these skills. Surveys of employers and expert commissions such as SCANS are one means to monitor such shifts, but they often must rely almost exclusively on judgment and opinion. There is a clear need for investment in job-validation studies, similar to those sponsored by the military, that link actual job performance with individual proficiency. Such studies conducted at meaningful intervals help ensure that lists of work-relevant competencies are developed not just on the basis of opinion but on the basis of systematic evidence.

performance with individual proficiency. Such studies conducted at meaningful intervals help ensure that lists of work-relevant competencies are developed not just on the basis of opinion but on the basis of systematic evidence.

EQUITY: RESOURCES, DEMOGRAPHICS, AND STUDENTS AT RISK

The panel suggests three main concepts with respect to equity (see

Figure 9

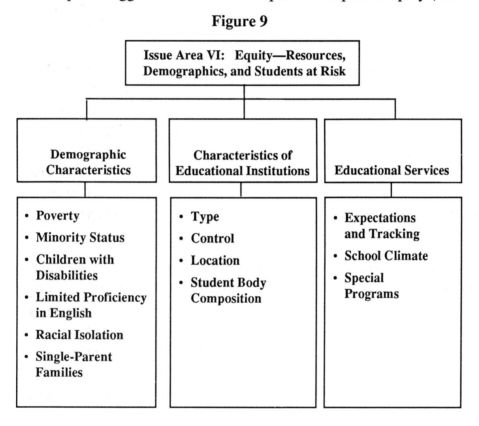

Figure 9).
- the demographic characteristics of students;
- the basic characteristics of educational institutions; and
- adequacy of educational services.

Demographic Characteristics of Students

The number of children at risk of educational failure for different reasons varies from state to state and can change over time as populations change. The number includes:

- children living in poverty and, in particular, in low-income, single-parent homes;

- minority youngsters—a group that is growing faster than the general population due, in part, to immigration and differential fertility rates;

- children with various physical and mental disabilities;

- children with limited English proficiency (LEP), including both those whose native language is not English and those speaking non-standard English; and

- children attending schools with high concentrations of students from poverty backgrounds.

The panel believes the nation needs regular reports on basic demographic characteristics of students, including cross-tabulations by gender, age, ethnic group, and socioeconomic background. The importance of disaggregating large data sets by important demographic characteristics cannot be overstated. Cross-tabulations of the sort

---

LOW PERFORMANCE AND DROPOUTS

Large dropout-rate differences among whites, blacks, and Hispanics grow smaller, vanish, or reverse themselves when such characteristics as family background or location of residence are taken into account. In fact, among students with low test scores, minority students are less likely than whites to drop out. Overall, 19 percent of the students whose scores were in the bottom quartile (three-fourths of the students had higher scores) dropped out of high school; 22 percent of all whites, 17 percent of all Hispanics, and 16 percent of all blacks in the bottom quartile dropped out. Similarly, blacks and whites living in the suburbs do not differ from one another in the dropout rates; nor do those living in central cities.

Source: Jeanne E. Griffith, Mary E. Frase, and John H. Ralph, "American Education: The Challenge of Change." Washington: Population Reference Bureau, Inc., 1989. (PRB Population Bulletin, Volume 44, No. 4, December 1989.)

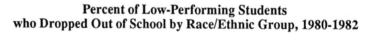

**Percent of Low-Performing Students
who Dropped Out of School by Race/Ethnic Group, 1980-1982**

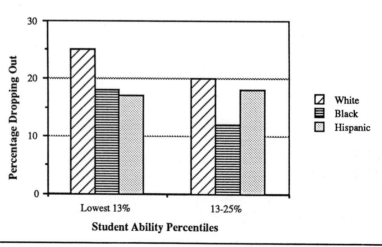

In addition, we need to know how many at-risk students are in our schools and colleges. How may have dropped out? How many have returned to education through "second chance" programs such as Job Corps, the GED diploma, or adult literacy efforts? Policymakers and educators also need much better data on the educational attainment of parents, particularly mothers, mobility of minority and at-risk youngsters from school to school, and the extent of racial isolation in the nation's schools, e.g., the proportion of minority students attending elementary or secondary schools in which 75 percent or more of the students are members of minority groups.

Implementation of this main concept requires, for example, monitoring the numbers and proportions of students enrolled in racially isolated schools, who come from single-parent families, who lack proficiency in standard English, or who come from low-income families. These factors apply to postsecondary as well as precollegiate students, although with some variation in focus. Parental educational attainment rather than single-parent status might be the more relevant indicator at the postsecondary level.

Educational Institutions

In addition to tracking numbers and demographic characteristics of students, it is important to monitor the institutions these students attend. The following key indicator areas are recommended:
- type (e.g., elementary, secondary, or community college);
- control—public, private;
- location—state; urban, rural, or suburban; and
- racial, ethnic, and socioeconomic composition of student body.

This main concept will provide useful information in a number of important areas. But it offers a particular opportunity to explore one of the most puzzling education phenomena of recent years. By 1976-77, the proportion of black high school graduates enrolling in colleges and universities in the United States equalled, for all intents and purposes, the proportion of white high school graduates enrolled. Since that time, this progress has collapsed for reasons that are not entirely understood. Have universities since 1975 altered their admissions standards in ways that discriminate against minority

Do students at risk have access to the full range of educational opportunities?

youngsters? Have costs of attendance so far outstripped increases in financial assistance that the door of the university is effectively shut in the faces of low-income youngsters, particularly low-income, minority students? Are the careers and financial rewards available in the volunteer military so attractive for black and other minority high school graduates that the expenditure of time, money, and foregone income involved in a college education is scarcely worth the effort? Or are other factors involved? The truth is that nobody knows and this concept area offers the opportunity to begin to explore these questions.

Services

Major elements of Issue Area 2 (Quality of Educational Institutions) should be developed around major equity concerns. In particular, we need to know if students at risk have access to the full range of educational opportunities, what kinds of learning opportunities are provided, and how well-tailored they are to the educational needs of these students. For example, it would be helpful to be able to report teacher qualifications and experience by the economic and ethnic composition of schools. Are the most experienced and most highly-qualified teachers found in low-income schools or in upper-income neighborhoods?

Expectations. A considerable body of small-scale research studies indicates that tracking and teacher expectations sort many minority students into less demanding curriculum very early in their school lives. Decisions about ability grouping can very easily be made in the first week of the child's entry into school and the consequences can last a lifetime. A significant aspect of monitoring the extent of tracking and ability grouping involves attending to the backgrounds and attitudes of teachers, both majority and minority, their experience in dealing with students from different backgrounds, and their training to work with at-risk students.

School Climate. Leaders of the "effective schools" movement of the 1970s argued that effective schools are characterized by such things as a strong leader (principal), high expectations for student performance, "a good school climate," and monitoring student performance and progress. "Good school climate" is difficult to assess, but this sub-construct should attempt to explore the extent to which every adult in the school begins with the proposition that "in this school, everyone can learn," an attitude that should be reinforced by administrators insisting that academic achievement is the school's highest priority.

Special Programs. Following years of debate, there now appears to be consensus that several school and preschool efforts—including Head Start and compensatory programs during the school year and the summer—produce definable, lasting, and long-term benefits to the populations they serve. Here we need to know how many students, of which kinds, have access to what kinds of services. What proportion of students eligible under Chapter 1 of the federal Elementary and Secondary Education Act are actually served? How are LEP children served in school—in bilingual programs or "immersion" efforts in English—and what are the effects on their achievement levels? To what extent are at-risk youngsters—including minority students, those with limited ability in English, and those with disabilities—provided services appropriate to their needs? Are these services provided in the regular classroom, or are the students "pulled" from the class for special efforts?

Implications for Indicators

As in several of the other issue areas, considerable information is available for some of the main concepts in this issue area. For

- CPS data include educational attainment (high school dropout, graduate, in high school, in college, college graduate) for 18-24-year-olds cross-indexed by family income.
- CPS data include similar enrollment data by ethnic group.
- Data are available on minority enrollment in higher education both by number and as a proportion of high school graduates.
- The Department of Education collects data on the dropout rates for persons with disabilities, aged 16 through 21, by disability, and NCES's NLS study has collected detailed data on the transition of people with disabilities from high school into postsecondary education and employment.
- Census data make it possible to examine students with limited English proficiency who have dropped out of high school and to break down dropout data on Hispanic students into specific ethnic subgroups (e.g., Mexican-American and Puerto Rican).
- NAEP provides ethnic breakdowns as part of every set of test results it releases and often reports on achievement results by level of parental education, type of community the

school serves, and the proportion of minority enrollment in the school.

- The College Board provides college-entrance test results disaggregated by ethnic group and sex.

Much more attention is needed to issues of equity in data collection and reporting.

The availability of this kind of information is helpful, but the panel believes much more attention is needed to issues of equity in data collection and reporting. The panel has already commented on the difficulty of accurately defining the true number of low-income children attending specific schools. But other problems in this area are equally serious. For example, sampling to ensure that at-risk students are not overlooked deserves serious attention from NCES. Some individuals, families, or schools may need to be oversampled. There are many examples of analyses that cannot be completed because particular subgroups, within a general sample, are not adequately represented. Several multiple analyses of CPS data—such as the proportion of Hispanic, single-parent families with children in preschool—cannot be conducted because of sample size. Of 900 schools in the High School and Beyond data set, only about 50 enroll a student body that is more than 50 percent poor. Many critics believe that the NAEP sample of urban minority students is too small for meaningful analyses.

For these reasons, it is critical that considerations of educational equity be designed into the indicator information system from the outset; they cannot work well as afterthoughts.

APPENDICES

APPENDIX A
Acknowledgments

The panel is grateful for the contributions of many individuals and organizations whose assistance made this report possible.

We want first to express our appreciation to several members of the panel who formed a writing group to help develop this document: Anthony S. Bryk, Leigh Burstein, Dennis P. Jones, Duncan MacRae, Jr., Arthur G. Powell, and Floraline I. Stevens. The writing group helped the panel develop its thinking about issue areas and drafted much of Part II of this report.

Our second acknowledgment goes to the NCES staff which helped us in our work. Study Director John Ralph was tireless in his commitment to this effort, a ready source of substance, ideas, and data, and a patient guide who helped keep the panel focused on its objectives.

A special word of thanks is due to Mary Moore (Mathematica Policy Research, Inc., Washington, D.C.), Brenda Turnbull (Policy Studies Associates, Washington, D.C.), and James Harvey (James Harvey & Associates, Washington, D.C.) for the substantive support they provided the panel. Ms. Moore and Ms. Turnbull brought considerable intelligence and informed judgment to our work on each of the issue areas. Mr. Harvey helped the panel draft and edit this report.

We also appreciate the work of the Washington Consulting Group (WCG) which under the direction of vice president Cyrus Baghelai provided support services to the Commission. Julie Czarnecki's efforts on behalf of the panel greatly eased our work; she organized every meeting we held over a two-year period, effortlessly and efficiently solving innumerable logistical and communications problems. We are also grateful for the effective help of WCG's Patrick Hill, Martine Brizius, and Lois Peak.

Several others also provided assistance at various points in the panel's existence: David Myers, Justin Boesel, and Robin Horn (Decision Resources Corporation, Washington, D.C.); Leslie Anderson, Heather McCollum, Daniel Spiro, and Margaret C. Thompson (Policy Studies Associates); Anne Milne (Anne Milne Associates, Washington, D.C.), Jim Crouse (University of Delaware), and Paul Mertins and Suellen Mauchamer (NCES).

APPENDIX B
Background Papers

*(These papers are available on request from the Data Development Division,
National Center for Education Statistics)*

James Crouse University of Delaware	Developing an Employment Readiness Indicator
Chester E. Finn, Jr. Vanderbilt University	What Good are International Indicators Anyway?
James Guthrie University of California-Berkeley	Should there be a "Dow Jones" Index for America's Schools: The Pros and Cons of Indicators for American Education
Robin Horn Decision Resources Corporation	Four Job Skills Gap Indicators
Mary Moore Mathematica Policy Research, Inc.	Issue Brief: Acquisition, Appreciation of, and Engagement in Subject Matter, Advanced Academic Thinking, and Citizenship Skills
	Issue Brief: Societal Support for Schools and Learning
	Issue Brief: Educational Contributions to Economic Productivity
Richard Rockwell Social Science Research Council	Lessons from the History of the Social Indicators Movement
Laura Salganik Pelavin Associates	Adjusting Educational Outcome Measures for Student Background: Strategies Used by States and a National Example
Ramsay W. Selden Council of Chief State School Officers	State Indicator Systems in Education
Brenda Turnbull Policy Studies Associates	Issue Brief: Quality of Schools and Educational Experiences
	Issue Brief: Readiness for School
	Issue Brief: Educational Equity for Children At Risk of School and Societal Failure
Brenda Turnbull and Heather McCollum Policy Studies Associates	Education Indicators
David Meyers and Robin Horn Decision Resources Corporation	Common Factors in the Development of Economic Indicators: Lessons Learned
Larry E. Suter, NCES and Joel D. Sherman, Pelavin Associates	International Indicators: Current Status and Future Prospects

APPENDIX C
Invited Guests and Speakers

John Bishop
Professor, Department of Human Resources

Jomills Braddock
Director, Center for Disadvantaged Students
Johns Hopkins University

Mike Cohen
Director of Education Policy Group
National Governors' Association

Christopher T. Cross
Assistant Secretary
Office of Educational Research and Improvement

Emerson Elliott
Acting Commissioner
National Center for Education Statistics

Joyce Epstein
Director, Effective Middle Schools Program
Johns Hopkins University

Robert Falb, Legislative Director
Office of Representative Peter Visclosky
Indiana

Pat Forgione, Chair
National Education Statistics Agenda Committee
National Forum on Education Statistics

Jeanne Griffith
Associate Commissioner for Data Development
National Center for Education Statistics

Nancy L. Karweit
Center for Social Organization of Schools
Johns Hopkins University

Birdie Kyle, Legislative Director
Office of Representative Nick Rahall
West Virginia

Milbrey W. McLaughlin
Professor, School of Education
Stanford University

Daniel Melnick, Division Director
Division of Science Resource Studies
National Science Foundation

Bob Stoltz
Director of Education Policy
Southern Regional Education Board

Dena Stoner, Executive Director
Council for Educational Development and Research

Richard Murnane
Professor of Education
Harvard Graduate School of Education

C. Robert Pace
Professor, Graduate School of Education
University of California, Los Angeles

Gary Phillips
Acting Associate Commissioner
Education Assessment Division
National Center for Education Statistics

Senta Raizen
Co-Director
National Center for Improving Science Education

Craig Ramey, Director
Civitan International Research Center
University of Alabama

Ted Sanders
Undersecretary
Department of Education

Jack Schwille, Assistant Dean
International Studies in Education
Michigan State University

Ramsay Selden, Director
State Education Assessment Center
Council of Chief State School Officers

Jack Shonkoff
Division of Development and Behavioral Sciences
University of Massachusetts Medical Center

Marshall Smith
Dean, School of Education
Stanford University

Joan Baratz-Snowden
Vice President for Assessment and Research
National Board for Professional Teaching Standards

Judith Torney-Purta
Professor of Human Development
University of Maryland